"An invigorating, practical, a flesh on the bones of theolog everywhere can tangibly live ... jesus spoke about. When you immerse yourself in these principles, you will discover a journey that surprises—and at times, confounds. But its goal is supremely worthwhile: an authentic, transformed life."

—**Stephan Bauman**, President, World Relief, author of *Possible*

"The principles underlined in these pages have made an impact on pastors and church leaders in Burundi and in the lives and ministries of ALARM leaders from 8 countries of east and central Africa. This is a key resource in our toolbox for transforming African Christianity from tribal to authentic biblical Christianity."

—**Reverend Célestin Musekura, Ph.D.**, President & Founder
African Leadership and Reconciliation Ministries, Inc.

"Grounded firmly in the Word of God and intensely practical, *Next Step Discipleship* will inspire new vision and bold action that will make a difference in your world. This is far more than a helpful guide for pastors. David Daniels provides invaluable insight to all believers with three vital steps in the Christian walk: *Belong, Become,* and *Beyond.* If you want to be used by God to reach across the street and around the world, read this book."

—**Dr. Ron Blue**, Adjunct Professor in World Missions
and Intercultural Studies, Dallas Theological Seminary

"*Next Step Discipleship* helps us go beyond our initial encounter with Jesus. Dr. Daniels will help you learn what it means to belong to Christ, what it means to grow in that relationship and then go beyond yourself as you encounter your neighbor....wherever that neighbor might be, from next door to across the world."

—**Mario Zandstra**, Regional Director of Redeemer City to City

"David Daniels has a huge heart for God and leaders, which is so apparent in these pages. He does a brilliant job of weaving together meaningful insights with practical application to empower leaders in any context. This is a resource the church needs around the world to help raise up and release a new generation of leaders."

—**Jud Wilhite**, Senior Pastor of Central Church, author of *Pursued*

# DAVID DANIELS

# NEXTSTEP
# DISCIPLESHIP

The Christian's Handbook
for Walking the Pathway
to Missional Living

# NEXTSTEP
# DISCIPLESHIP

*The Christian's Handbook for Walking
the Pathway to Missional Living*

David Daniels

PANTEGO**PUBLISHING**
*Ministry Resources by Pantego Bible Church*
Fort Worth, Texas, USA
2016

Published by Pantego Publishing
Pantego Bible Church
8001 Anderson Boulevard
Fort Worth, Texas 76120
www.pantego.org

First Printing 2016

Unless otherwise indicated, Scripture is taken from the Holy Bible, *New International Version*®, Copyright © 1984, 2001, 2010 by Biblica, Inc.™

*To Tiffany, who has proved with her life
that an enduring commitment to Jesus
yields beautiful fruit beyond.*

# CONTENTS

# WITH GRATITUDE

*In all my prayers for all of you, I always pray with joy because of
your partnership in the gospel from the first day until now.*
Philippians 1:4-5

Second Timothy 2:2 challenges, *"And the things you have heard me
say in the presence of many witnesses, entrust to reliable men who will also
be qualified to teach others."* I humbly recognize that whatever ministry
I have has been passed on to me by faithful people before me. I am
grateful for the leaders, mentors, counselors and helpers whom God
has used to shape my ministry for 26 years. I am especially indebted
to Dr. Rob Harrell, my spiritual mentor from the earliest years of my
new spiritual life. He entrusted ministry to me, giving me the first
opportunity to give myself away. I thank God for you!

While I was taking baby steps as a pastor, Gayle Greenwood
Clark and Cheryl Fletcher modelled deliberate and dedicated discipleship. You taught me what a missional disciple was before I even
understood what I was doing. Thank you for leading me, loving me
and then following me in some of the richest years of ministry.

Keith Smith, Executive Pastor at Pantego Bible Church, has been
my loyal friend. I am grateful for your patience, creativity and authenticity. You model what it means to truly love the flock of God.

Thanks to Dr. Tom Bulick, Spiritual Formation Pastor at Pantego
Bible Church, for your constant wisdom. You, along with the rest of
our Extended Leadership team (Teresa Boudreau, Kevin Glenn, Wen-
dy Hollabaugh, Ryan Rasberry, Jon Rhiddlehoover, Lupe Salazar,

Roger Sappington, Mac Shirley, Tim Tibbles and Toney Upton), have helped our church "live" this spiritual pathway through your shaping and sharpening advice.

Many thanks to leaders who have encouraged us to carry these principles beyond Pantego Bible Church: Dr. Célestin Musekura, Deogratias Nshiyimana and Jean Baptiste of African Leadership and Reconciliation Ministries; Method Bigirimana of our ReGenesis Church in Fort Worth; and Pastor Andrew Dev in India.

Stann Leff, my faithful mentor from Minnesota, has stood on the sidelines of my ministry, cheering me on with great enthusiasm. I appreciate your strong affirmation and refusal to hang up the phone without praying for me, my family and my church.

Thanks, Alison Dellenbaugh, for your sharp editing skills and ever-constant encouragement to write what's in my heart. Thank you for using your gifts for Christ's church and the nations. Melanie Butts and Manny Fernandez also gave their valuable time editing initial drafts. And, Dr. Bruce Hurt and Jeff and Barbara Loomis afforded me beautiful retreats on the coast and in Austin to write such a work. Your hospitality has been unwavering for 30 years.

Finally, to my sweet bride, Tiffany, I give my deepest gratitude. Not only have you been a perfect helpmate, but you have modeled the spiritual pathway better than anyone I know. In you, I see a deep love for Jesus and His church, a life of genuine transformation and a missional heart to help others come into the Kingdom. I and our children—Grant (and wife, Laine), Pearson and Jenna—always learn from your godly life and are led to be disciples, changed by God to change our world.

# ON THE ROAD TO MISSION

*I consider my life worth nothing to me, if only I may finish the race
and complete the task the Lord Jesus has given me—the task
of testifying to the gospel of God's grace.*
Acts 20:24

The shortest route from Dallas, Texas to Fayetteville, Arkansas takes about five and a half hours by car. It took me eight.

We scheduled an afternoon for my daughter to tour The University of Arkansas as a potential college choice after high school graduation. Several days earlier, I went online to book a hotel room "near the University of Arkansas" and, on our travel date, simply entered the hotel address into my phone GPS. How was I supposed to know that the University of Arkansas apparently has a remote branch in *Little Rock*...more than two hours south of where we needed to be!? I drove to the right place in the wrong direction. Some would say that we took "the scenic route," but we finally arrived.

For me, the road to missional discipleship hasn't been a direct one. God has taken me along the scenic route to bring me to a greater understanding of His purpose for my life and for His church. Several key lessons have shaped me and have formed the foundation for my life as a disciple of Jesus and, eventually, for this book.

### Lesson #1: Strategic Discipleship

I graduated from Denver Seminary in 1993 and returned to Austin, Texas, to start my first pastorate at First Evangelical Free Church (now Austin Oaks Church). A year later, I accepted the opportunity to lead our college ministry—a fertile mission field in a city with more than 100,000 college students within reach. At that time, we had 30-40 collegiates attending a class on Sunday morning and a handful attending a mid-week Bible Study. Though I could see the fields were "white for harvest," I was still learning how to "farm."

Fortunately, the Lord provided two faithful servants to help me. Gayle Greenwood Clark had been serving on our church staff for several years, even raising her own salary support, because she believed college students were one of the best investments a church could make. Cheryl Fletcher served with a parachurch ministry, but gave her time and ministry insight as a volunteer to our students. Today, I'm still convinced that these two women were two of God's generous gifts to college students, and me, during that critical season.

Gayle and Cheryl demonstrated remarkable faithfulness to a disciplemaking vision during this time. They intentionally pursued students, challenged them, trained them and mobilized them to make a difference with their lives. I remember confessing to both that "I really wasn't sure what I was doing" when it came to making disciples. But Gayle and Cheryl became a living textbook to sharpen my ministry skills over the next 10 years.

One of the most important lessons I learned from these ministry partners was the value of developing an intentional strategy—in our growing ministry and with specific students. The principle is true: "If you aim at nothing, you'll hit it every time." We met frequently to consider how we might be more and more effective stewards of the time, resources and people entrusted to us. Rather than operate from a one-size-fits-all template, we worked to consider the uniqueness of each student and how we might strategically help them grow in their personal relationship with Jesus.

Over the next 10 years, ECHO, our college ministry, exploded. By 2003, almost 1000 students were meeting at our church for our student-led worship service. More than 100 discipleship groups had been formed and, each year, nearly 200 students were sent on short-term Spring Break and summer mission trips around the world. During that time, God gave us the privilege of training future pastors, missionaries, church planters, elders and teachers, not to mention the hundreds of business professionals who are making a difference with the Gospel in the marketplace today. Watching the Lord "change people to change their world" through our intentional, strategic efforts became the first stop on my journey of missional discipleship.

## Lesson #2: These Are Your People

In 2003, God called me to CrossPoint Church in Bloomington, Minnesota, to take the Senior Pastor role in a smaller congregation. Though the culture and climate were a shock to our southern-born systems, Tiffany and I connected in some treasured relationships. Today, I still stay in touch with Stann Leff, a former white-collar executive, who has been a shining example of how all Christians can leverage their God-given gifts and present circumstances to reach those who do not know Jesus and encourage those who do.

During my brief time in Minnesota, I learned many leadership lessons which would become indispensable for my ministry future. But, one missional lesson stood out among others: Every church exists, in part, for those people who are not there, but should be. God places His people in particular places at particular times (Acts 17:26-27) to participate in His grand mission. So, the people in the vicinity of our church are "our people," the ones we're called to reach.

Normandale Community College, the largest institution of its kind in the state, is right across the street from CrossPoint Church. Though we had a small handful of faithful adults who connected with international students at the college, we had little witness among the almost 10,000 others enrolled there. We were *their* church, but we failed to reach *our* people.

The blame for this neglect rests squarely on my leadership shoulders. While I was busy arranging the pieces of personnel, policies and programs, I missed the very missional purpose of the church: to reach unreached people with the glorious Gospel of Jesus. I eventually learned that this problem plagues more than a few churches today. We "step on dollars looking for dimes," so to speak, missing the very reason for our existence. And, if the local church doesn't champion a missional outreach among its neighbors, it shouldn't surprise anyone that the people *in the church* won't cultivate concern for their neighbors across the street, colleagues at work or friends at school.

### Lesson #3: Mission Is Worship

Through the providence of God, my family moved back to Texas for me to become Senior Pastor at Pantego Bible Church in 2005. Before I arrived, I was contacted by another church in the area asking me if I would teach the first lesson in a missions training course they were planning to offer months later. Perspectives on the World Christian Movement is an excellent 15-week intensive seminar designed to help Christians examine and embrace God's purposes in the world. I agreed to teach Lesson #1: "The Living God is a Missionary God," and, over the next several years, taught this biblical foundation in dozens of other venues.

While I was eager to teach others, God used my immersion in Perspectives Lesson #1 to radically shape my own missional heart. I was reminded of God's initial plan to magnify Himself through people designed to reflect His glory. I reflected on how sin abdicated God's reign and contaminated God's reflection in each person. I recalled how God's covenant with Abraham laid the foundation for God's redemptive work in Jesus Christ, first for Israel and then for the church. I remembered that the *Missio Dei* is ultimately the redemption of people for the glory of God and that worship and mission are inseparable. In the end, I determined that missions is not "one of the things a church does." It *is* what the church does! God had given me a new perspective.

It was time to put this perspective into practice.

### Lesson #4: Community For Mission

In those days, Pantego Bible Church was a church vibrant with biblical community. The former pastor had developed a ministry paradigm that encouraged people to "do life together," and a large portion of the church was connected in Home Groups, practicing spiritual formation, evangelism, volunteerism, recreation, international mission, local compassion and care for one another. This model is still a core tenet of the way we do church.

However, along the way, Pantego Bible Church had lost its focus on missions. Though the church had a rich history of sending and supporting missionaries, very little of its effort had been focused outwardly in recent years. The church had succeeded in loving one another at the expense of loving our neighbors.

With 10 years of making disciples among college students, the memory of a missed opportunity in my former church in Minnesota, and a biblical mandate of God's glory in global missions, I seized the opportunity to lead our church to missional discipleship. No longer were we just going to *go* to church; the time was long overdue to *be* the church to our neighbors and nations.

We changed our church mission statement to express this new commitment. I preached sermons specifically on the topics of social justice, personal evangelism and global impact. We formed international partnerships with our missionaries and forged short-term trips for our people, not just to send, but to go beyond our borders. In a move of daring faith, our elders agreed to cover the balance of any attendee who felt called to a short-term mission and worked hard to raise support, but came up short of their financial goal. In the next five years, no support gaps had to be bridged among the nearly 600 global travelers. God was blessing His missional church.

In 2009, I finished preaching our morning services when two men approached me and introduced themselves: Pastor January, his chosen American name, had recently arrived in the United States from a refugee camp in Tanzania, East Africa. His Burundian translator, Method Bigirimana, explained that they represented a congregation of resettled Africans living nearby in Fort Worth. They had attended the morning worship service and lingered to ask one question, "Do you have a place where our people might meet with God each week?" The nations were at our doorstep.

Over the next few weeks, we welcomed an African congregation to Pantego Bible Church. God used the connection of two unlikely congregations to stir our hearts and open our eyes with a global vision. Volunteers immediately started an "Essentials Closet" to provide basic hygiene and home care products not covered under the U.S. welfare assistance program. Every week, church attendees brought items such as soap, shampoo, laundry detergent and toothpaste for regular distribution to our African friends. Next, some at our church went through the necessary steps to become authorized ESL teachers. English classes met twice a week to teach language skills to help our friends move toward American citizenship. In time, our church responded to practical needs of refugee families by providing school supplies and backpacks at the beginning of each school year and gifts for children each Christmas. In the next several years, we began the delicate process of integrating English-speaking African children into our Sunday morning children's and student ministries in order to mainstream them into American culture. A group of women at our church began to gather home goods—towels, pots, plates and silverware, linens, lamps, etc.—to benefit each incoming refugee newcomer. And, finally, I and other pastors began to meet with the elders of this new church to understand their needs and train them in theological and leadership principles.

Our missional impact didn't stop there. Over the next few years, individuals and groups committed themselves to orphan and foster care, homeless outreach, ministry to adults with substance addictions and families of children with special needs. Over a three-year span, our church launched five new missionary families into global ministry. A school superintendent changed his life-course and started giving all of his time to serve those in poverty within our community. A woman sold her bakery to begin working with refugees. A corporate CEO and his wife began giving extravagantly to Bible translation around the world. A judge started traveling to Africa to give her legal expertise to war-torn communities. A young boy launched an initiative to provide scholarships to children escaping abusive homes.

We were finally fulfilling, not just *our* mission, but *God's* mission for His church. We were "making God known by making disciples who are changed by God to change their world." A major shift was happening at Pantego Bible Church: from comfortable community to community for the sake of radical mission. Our commitment to the mission of God for the glory of God has permeated virtually every dimension of our church. Today, we can't imagine *not* going beyond.

## An Invitation Beyond

As we learned principles for moving people from biblical community to biblical mission, we decided to share what we have learned with others. Leadership teams travelled to Africa to partner with African Leadership and Reconciliation Ministries (ALARM) to teach missional discipleship to church leaders there. The principles throughout this book have also been shared in Spain, Cuba and China, and we are expecting to share it with pastors in India. In 2015, I began writing my first book, *Next Step Church*, as a free ministry resource to train pastors in what you will learn as our "spiritual pathway." The goal was not primarily to publish another book for an American audience, but to equip missional leaders around the world.

Very quickly, it became apparent that an edited version of *Next Step Church* could be helpful to Christians everywhere. We also realized that a condensed version would be beneficial in teaching new members of Pantego Bible Church about our church history and strategic mission. This book was written for this purpose.

*Next Step Discipleship* is an invitation for you to join a journey. To be a missional disciple is to organize your life around God's great missional purposes. The lesson from my college ministry days is that discipleship is an intentional and strategic pursuit. From my Minnesota stint, we learn that people must seize the immediate opportunities to reach the people God has placed around them. The Perspectives course reminds us that missions exists for the glory of God. Missions is worship and this has been God's intent throughout all of history. And, the recent years at Pantego Bible Church give us a practical picture of the extravagant blessing and global impact of missional community. This commitment isn't just for our church. It isn't just for me. It's for every follower of Jesus.

My prayer is that the Lord uses this work to challenge and change any distorted ideas of church and the Christian life you might hold. As you explore the spiritual pathway described here, I trust the Lord will inspire you to connect in true biblical community with others. I hope you will experience spiritual transformation by the power of the Holy Spirit. And, ultimately, I earnestly desire for every disciple to consider their life not their own, but to run the race and finish the task of testifying to the Gospel of grace. I hope you will go beyond. And may God make Himself famous through you!

*Soli Deo Gloria*
David Daniels
September 2016

# 1

# THE SPIRITUAL PATHWAY

*Whether you turn to the right or to the left, your ears will hear*
*a voice behind you, saying, "This is the way; walk in it."*
Isaiah 30:21

I have been privileged to travel the world, training leaders and partnering with ministries in Russia, Estonia, Ukraine, China, Hong Kong, Spain, Ethiopia, Burundi, Rwanda, India, Cuba and Mexico. Each trip, I plan and book my own travel itinerary, working to get the most economical ticket with the shortest route. Each time, I must know two pieces of information: where I am and where I am going. If I don't know where I am, I won't know where to start. And, if I don't know where I'm going, I could end up *anywhere*! But, if I'm sure of both, the airline is able to coordinate a very specific route for me to get to my destination.

This book is a travel guide to help you discover the spiritual pathway for your life. This pathway assumes that you are at a particular place in your spiritual journey right now and it assumes that God has an intended route for you to follow with an intended destination for you to reach. The question is, what route will take you from where you are along the path to missional living?

The Bible frequently uses the idea of a "path" or a "way" to refer to the spiritual journey. We are sometimes commanded to "walk" in a particular way or to stay on the narrow road. This is a small sampling of these themes in the Bible:

*Direct me in the path of your commands, for there I find delight.* (Psalm 119:35)

*Whether you turn to the right or to the left, your ears will hear a voice behind you, saying, "This is the way; walk in it."* (Isaiah 30:21)

*This is what the Lord says: "Stand at the crossroads and look; ask for the ancient paths, ask where the good way is, and walk in it, and you will find rest for your souls."* (Jeremiah 6:16)

*He has shown you, O mortal, what is good. And what does the Lord require of you? To act justly and to love mercy and to walk humbly with your God.* (Micah 6:8)

*Trust in the LORD with all your heart and lean not on your own understanding; in all your ways acknowledge him, and he will make your paths straight.* (Proverbs 3:5-6)

*Show me your ways, O LORD, teach me your paths; guide me in your truth and teach me, for you are God my Savior, and my hope is in you all day long.* (Psalm 25:4-5)

*LORD, you have assigned me my portion and my cup; you have made my lot secure. The boundary lines have fallen for me in pleasant places; surely I have a delightful inheritance...You have made known to me the path of life...* (Psalm 16:5-6, 11)

*There is a way which seems right to a man, but in the end leads to death.* (Proverbs 14:12)

*He who strays from the path of understanding comes to rest in the company of the dead.* (Proverbs 21:16)

*Your word is a lamp for my feet, a light on my path.* (Psalm 119:105)

*So I say, walk by the Spirit, and you will not gratify the desires of the flesh.* (Galatians 5:16)

*"Come follow Me," Jesus said...* (Matthew 4:19)

*"I am the way, the truth and the life..."* (John 14:6)

A "pathway" that we are to follow or "walk" appears as a consistent theme in Scripture. So, the role of the pastor and the goal of the church is to move people along the "spiritual pathway" to deeper life with God.

The problem is that most people have no direction and most churches have no destination. If you ask a Christian, "Where are you right now in your spiritual journey?" most will have no idea how to evaluate their present condition. Or, if you asked, "Where are you going in your spiritual journey?" most Christians would answer, "I'm going to heaven," as if eternity is the only goal of the spiritual life. Many churches contribute to this lack of direction by not giving people a definitive pathway for living their spiritual life. The dangerous and deceptive result is that the church's measure of discipleship is: busyness. The more activities church members participate in, the more mature they must be.

This was never God's plan.

Busy people are not necessarily better people. A schedule filled with activity doesn't automatically produce disciples filled with the Holy Spirit. And, a church with programs may never see Christians make progress along the pathway toward spiritual maturity.

What this book proposes is a specific, but simple, spiritual pathway for any church. At Pantego Bible Church, we have experienced tremendous success in seeing our people move along the pathway toward missional living. This pathway is described by three steps: Belong, Become and Beyond.

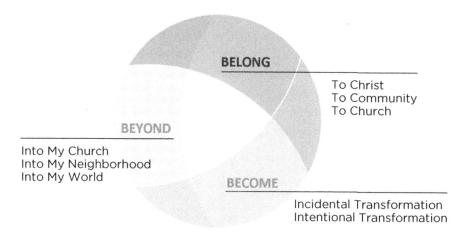

**BELONG**

To Christ
To Community
To Church

BEYOND

Into My Church
Into My Neighborhood
Into My World

BECOME

Incidental Transformation
Intentional Transformation

## STEP #1: A PLACE TO BELONG

The first step along the spiritual pathway is to BELONG—the step of connection. It's a place of interpersonal relationships. Every Christian begins their journey with God by first belonging to Jesus Christ. Next, they connect to a biblical community of people where they can do life together. Finally, every Christian needs to belong to a church, a corporate Body where they partner with a larger mission. To summarize, to BELONG is to connect with...

- Jesus Christ, through faith in Him
- Biblical community, for life together
- A local church, to partner with the mission

## STEP #2: A PLACE TO BECOME

The second step along the spiritual pathway is to BECOME—the step of transformation by the Holy Spirit. It's not a physical place, but the state of ongoing spiritual maturity. As we will learn later, many Christians do not experience much of the life change that God intends for them. In this step, the Christian longs for greater sanctification and trusts God for greater growth as they BECOME the person God intends for them to be.

## STEP #3: A PLACE BEYOND

The third step along the spiritual pathway is to go BEYOND—the step of mission. It's a place of purpose and action. In this step, the Christian is compelled by the mission of God to go beyond their current job, routine, community, etc., to wherever God calls them. It is important for every Christian to serve beyond themselves in their local church, using their spiritual gifts to build the Body. The Christian goes beyond into their local community, believing that God placed them where they live for a strategic purpose (Acts 17:26-27). Finally, the Christian embraces God's global mission to go beyond into the world. To summarize, going BEYOND means giving my life...

- In my church
- In my community
- In my world

There are several reasons why this model is so effective:

**The pathway is simple.** It is easy for pastors to communicate and easy for people to understand. Moreover, it is a simple tool by which the church may plan and evaluate its ministries and people may evaluate their own lives.

**The pathway is intentional.** The spiritual pathway has a particular goal: not to grow a church, but to produce missional disciples. This pathway will enable you to take personal responsibility for cultivating spiritual growth in your life. Each step offers the opportunity for you to be deliberate in your walk with Jesus.

**The pathway is progressive.** It keeps people moving forward toward increasing spiritual maturity and mission. Frequently, Christians feel like they are "running in circles," not making any progress. This pathway looks forward to a "next step" of growth each time. Once a person connects in relationships and BELONGS to Jesus and community, their next expected step is to pursue life change. If a person is BECOMING more like Jesus, they are being changed to change their world (BEYOND).

It important at this point to note that growing disciples don't "graduate" from one step to another. As people BELONG to Jesus and community, they begin the journey to BECOME more like Jesus. But, they don't cease connecting to Jesus or their community. In fact, their increasing life change (BECOME) will likely deepen their connection with Jesus and other believers. In the same way, as a Christian begins to go BEYOND on mission, they don't leave life change behind. In reality, each missional venture will most assuredly produce even greater life change. The pathway is cyclical, enabling the maturing disciple to grow deeper and deeper in connection, transformation and mission over a lifetime.

**The pathway is reproductive.** It doesn't have a final end. The end of mission (BEYOND) is that new converts are made who, in turn, BELONG to Jesus, community and the church. Then, as they BECOME more like Jesus and go BEYOND into their community and world, they make more converts who likewise repeat the process. This is a model of spiritual multiplication.

**The pathway is personal.** This isn't a plan just for the local church. It's a developmental plan for individuals. When people understand each step, they are able to personally assess where they are and where they should go "next."

The rest of this book will take each of the steps along the spiritual pathway and explain them for the follower of Jesus wishing to grow toward greater missional discipleship. Occasionally, it will be helpful for you to ask "Where am I?" as you think about each step along the pathway. Hopefully, as you apply these biblical principles, you will enjoy greater spiritual fruit and will have greater spiritual impact in your community and the world beyond.

In each of the next chapters, the following diagram will remind you where you are on the spiritual pathway:

| BELONG | | | BECOME | | BEYOND | | |
|---|---|---|---|---|---|---|---|
| TO CHRIST | TO COMMUNITY | TO CHURCH | INCIDENTAL TRANSFORMATION | INTENTIONAL TRANSFORMATION | INTO MY CHURCH | INTO MY NEIGHBORHOOD | INTO MY WORLD |

## TAKE THE NEXT STEP

1. How would you respond if someone asked you, "Where are you?" or "Where are you going?"

2. What does the word "Belong" bring to mind for you? Why do you think this word is important for the disciple of Jesus?

3. What does the word "Become" bring to mind for you? Why do you think this word is important for the disciple of Jesus?

4. What does the word "Beyond" bring to mind for you? Why do you think this word is important for the disciple of Jesus?

5. What is the most important thing you learned from this chapter?

# BELONG: TO CHRIST

*And you also are among those who*
*are called to belong to Jesus Christ.*
Romans 1:6

I met Jesus in 1983. I grew up in a religious family, attended church almost every Sunday and learned a religious catechism. But I had no spiritual connection to Jesus until I heard the Gospel and responded in faith at 17 years old. At that time, I was adopted into the family of God. My relationship with God changed. I "belonged" to Him (Romans 1:6).

Nowhere does the Bible teach that all people are "children of God." In fact, the Bible states that all people are sinners (Romans 3:23), separated from God (Ephesians 2:12), enemies of Jesus (Philippians 3:18), lawless rebels (Titus 2:14) and haters of God (Romans 1:30). This is our natural, human condition. We only become children of God through faith in Jesus Christ (Galatians 3:26). At conversion we become "a people belonging to God" (1 Peter 2:9) and a "people for His own possession" (Titus 2:14). This is the first step of any person's spiritual journey. It is the step to BELONG.

How do we take this first step in our spiritual journey?

| BELONG | | | BECOME | | BEYOND | | |
|---|---|---|---|---|---|---|---|
| TO CHRIST | TO COMMUNITY | TO CHURCH | INCIDENTAL TRANSFORMATION | INTENTIONAL TRANSFORMATION | INTO MY CHURCH | INTO MY NEIGHBORHOOD | INTO MY WORLD |

## Beware of a Wrong Gospel

For sinners to be saved, they must hear and respond to the Gospel of Jesus. The Gospel means "good news." Jesus has died as a substitute for sinners so human beings may live eternally with God. Unfortunately, the Gospel has been distorted many times so that, even in Christ's church, a false Gospel is preached.

In Acts 20:29-31, Paul predicted this would happen:

*I know that after I leave, savage wolves will come in among you and will not spare the flock. Even from your own number men will arise and distort the truth in order to draw away disciples after them. So be on your guard! Remember that for three years I never stopped warning each of you night and day with tears.*

Wolves in sheep's clothing would invade the church, distort the truth and lead unsuspecting people away from Jesus and toward the false teachers. With passionate urgency, Paul begs the church to stand guard.

Later, in the apostle's letter to the churches in Galatia, he alerts Christians that his prediction had come true. He writes, "*I am astonished that you are so quickly deserting the one who called you by the grace of Christ and are turning to a different gospel—which is really no gospel at all. Evidently some people are throwing you into confusion and are trying to pervert the gospel of Christ*" (Galatians 1:6-7). The word "deserted" means "to change sides." Christians who had sided with the true Gospel of grace switched to the side of error and began following a different gospel, which Paul adds "is really no gospel at all." Paul condemns the false teachers for promoting such lies and warns people that they are in danger by following them.

On more than one occasion, I've heard a news story of a person wanting to get discounted concert tickets. They shop online and find a seller offering tickets for 50% or more off the original ticket price. After the tickets have been purchased and printed, the customer presents their ticket at the concert only to discover that the ticket is a counterfeit. The buyer has been duped and is not allowed entrance to the event because what they possess isn't what is required.

Jesus warned that many will come to the door of the Kingdom of

God and say, "Lord, Lord" ("Master"), but will be turned away because they have bought into a counterfeit gospel (Matthew 7:21-23). They have believed a false gospel such as:

- The Gospel of Works—believing that my best moral efforts and genuine intentions make me right with God.
- The Gospel of Denominationalism—believing that membership in a particular denomination gains a person better standing with God.
- The Gospel of Covenantalism—believing that a person is automatically a Christian if their parents are Christian.
- The Gospel of Baptism—believing baptism is necessary for salvation.
- The Gospel of Universalism—believing that God is so loving that He automatically forgives everyone and offers everyone heaven.
- The Gospel of Second Chances—believing that all people will get a second chance to believe after they die.

We must be on guard against these false "gospels." A false gospel is any teaching about righteousness which causes hearers to take their eyes off the cross of Jesus and put their hope in anything else. Just as the devil did in the Garden of Eden with Adam and Eve, he distorts truth, twists the commands of God and presents his own kind of truth—which isn't truth at all. Satan "masquerades as an angel of light" (2 Corinthians 11:14). If works, denominations, family pedigree, baptism or anything else become part of a person's standing before God, they are trusting in a different Gospel than the gospel of Jesus—one which is really no Gospel at all.

## Believe the Right Gospel

The Bible is a big book with many helpful principles for the spiritual life. Woven throughout its pages is a simple story of the Gospel. Since the day I first heard this Gospel, I have thought about it as series of progressive "movements" or spiritual truths. Take your time reading the next few pages and ask yourself whether you have believed the right Gospel.

## TRUTH #1: Our Problem is Sin
*...for all have sinned and fall short of the glory of God.*
Romans 3:23

All human beings are sinners (Romans 3:9-20, 23). This is a fact describing our spiritual condition passed down from our father Adam. There is no one who does not sin (1 Kings 8:46). Not only is sin a universal problem, it is also an ungodly one. In other words, sin is fundamentally a disposition *against* God. It is lawlessness, rebellion and hatred toward the things of God. And, once this ungodliness entered the world, it distorted human beings made in the image of God, contaminating our intellect, relationships, emotions, will, ethics and bodies. We were created in God's image to reflect His glory, but as sinners we no longer do what we were designed to do.

## TRUTH #2: Our Penalty is Death
*For the wages of sin is death, but the gift of God is*
*eternal life in Christ Jesus our Lord.*
Romans 6:23

The wage for sin, or what we have earned, is death. This death isn't just the end of life after we grow old. Death comes in several forms for the person who doesn't belong to God. First, sin produces a death of freedom so that we become enslaved. Sin traps us and becomes a ruthless master over our lives (Romans 6:20). Second, sin produces a death of innocence so that we become guilty before God, without excuse for our disobedience (Romans 6:21). Finally, and most significantly, sin produces a death in our relationship with God. Because God is holy, He will not compromise His character and tolerate unholiness. Just as Adam and Eve were cast out of the Garden and God's presence, so our sin creates a chasm between us and God now and forever. A person who is living today without Jesus Christ is really dead.

## TRUTH #3: Our Provision is Christ
*But God demonstrates his own love for us in this:*
*While we were still sinners, Christ died for us.*
Romans 5:8

None of us can overcome the death grip of sin. No matter what good works we try to perform, the residue of sin remains. We may be able to disguise sin, but we cannot undo sin. Fortunately, God saw humans in their helplessness and did for us what we could never do for ourselves. He sent His Son, Jesus, to take our sin on Himself and die in our place. He became our substitution, bearing our penalty on the cross and offering us forgiveness and life with God. The sacrifice of Jesus is sometimes described as a "great exchange:" *"God made Him who knew no sin to become sin for us so that in Him, we might become the righteousness of God"* (2 Corinthians 5:21). Jesus' death was a demonstration of God's love and was offered before we could ever do anything good (Romans 5:8, John 3:16). Jesus Christ is God's free gift for redeeming and restoring our relationship with Him.

## TRUTH #4: Our Profession is Faith

*That if you confess with your mouth, "Jesus is Lord," and believe in your heart that God raised him from the dead, you will be saved.*
Romans 10:9

Eternal life is a free gift from God, but is received through the response of personal faith. When a person understands the work of Jesus for them and trusts that Jesus was the living Son of God (not just a great prophet or teacher), they surrender their life to Him in faith and invite Him to take control of their life. In this moment of faith, a sinner becomes a child of God, adopted into His family, forgiven and set free. This is the moment of belonging.

These four simple truths are the Gospel of Jesus. The bad news is that we are all sinners under the penalty of death. The good news is that God has sent His Son into the world to die in our place, and we may trust Him for eternal life. Believe no other Gospel.

I encourage you to stop reading and ask yourself, "Where am I?" Where are you in regard to a relationship with God? Are you confident that you have eternal life? Have you placed your faith in Jesus alone for the forgiveness of your sins? If not, and you believe what you have just read, you may offer your heartfelt prayer to God and receive eternal life:

*Dear God, I believe I am a sinner and Jesus alone is my Savior. I trust that He is the Son of God who took my sin to reconcile me with You. I place my faith in Him and welcome Him into my life. Change my life and help me live for you. Thank You for eternal life! Amen.*

## Tell Your Story

In 1866, Arabelle Hankey wrote the lyrics to the hymn "I Love to Tell the Story." The simple chorus is beautiful:

*I love to tell the story, 'twill be my theme in glory,*
*To tell the old, old story of Jesus and His love.*

The theme of every conversation and song in eternity will be the marvelous grace of God, demonstrated through the loving sacrifice of His Son for helpless sinners. We should tell the story today as often as we can! Unfortunately, many Christians do not know how to tell their story—the unique testimony of how and when they trusted Jesus Christ. In 1 Peter 3:15, the Scriptures urge the Christian, *"Always be prepared to give an answer to everyone who asks you to give the reason for the hope that you have."* The Christian must be prepared to share their personal story of hope.

We may think of the Christian's testimony as having three parts or "chapters": Before, How and After. The first part gives a brief description of what your life was like before trusting in Jesus. Highlight your search for meaning, your attempt to do good or the emptiness you might have felt. Next, explain how you encountered Jesus. Where did you hear the message of the Gospel? What did God reveal to you? What Bible verse impacted you the most? This is the moment where you express the reality of sin and the sacrifice of Jesus on the cross. Finally, express what your life has been like since your conversion. Honestly admit that you aren't perfect, but share how you are growing in the knowledge of God.

Write your testimony out. Edit and rewrite. Remember, this is the most important story that will ever be told. Craft a story that explains your conversion in rich detail and practice sharing it. Create a much shorter version—3-5 minutes—that can be told at a moment's notice. Both your testimony and the Gospel "movements" are two indispensable tools for your ministry.

I have shared my own personal testimony hundreds of times and am always encouraged to reflect on the work of God in my life. Here is my brief story, posted here to help the reader see the movements of "Before," "How" and "After."

## BEFORE

*I was raised in a very religious family, going to church almost every Sunday and being trained in Sunday School from an early age. But, while I was part of a church, saw images of the cross and heard Bible stories, I never understood who Jesus is or what He did for me.*

*My relationship with parents and brothers was sometimes strained, often because of me and especially as I grew into my teenage years. I described myself as the "black sheep" of the family…a high achiever at school, but never feeling like I could please others. I struggled with a deep sense of inadequacy and searched for personal affirmation in my studies, drama performances and my abilities as an artist. I longed to be loved and accepted.*

## HOW

*A month before my high school graduation, I had another of what had become frequent arguments with my parents. I left home and drove to the retail store where my best friend, Robert, and I were employed as assistant managers. It was closing time and, as I helped him sweep the stockroom floor, my friend asked me two questions that would forever change my life. Sensing my despair, Robert asked, "David, if you were to die tonight, how sure are you that you would spend eternity with God?"*

*I answered, "I feel very sure." Remember, I was a very religious person.*

*Robert then asked the second question, "And, if you were to stand before God, what reason would you give as to why you should spend eternity with Him?"*

*I arrogantly replied, "Because I'm better than my brothers." Yes, that was my answer! But, it revealed my serious misunderstanding of what it means to belong to God. I believed that I simply needed to be better than most people to go to heaven. But, my friend shared four truths that corrected my religious misunderstanding.*

*First, Robert told me that all people were sinners, including me. I accepted this because I knew there were some things that I had done that definitely displeased God.*

*Second, he told me that the "wages of sin is death" (Romans 6:23). Just as employees must be paid for the work they perform, so sinners must be "paid" the wages of sin. And, what is owed to all of us because of our sin is death—eternal separation from God.*

*Third, Robert told me that none of us can do anything to remedy our sin problem. We cannot go to church, give to charity or clean up our lives. Because, no matter how good we might be from this point forward, the residue of sin will always remain. Only Jesus Christ can take away sin. God sent His Son, Jesus Christ, into the world to live a perfect life and then die a death He didn't deserve in order to pay a penalty than none of us could afford. He laid down His life for me! Romans 5:8 states, "But God demonstrates His own love for us in that while we were yet sinners, Christ died for us." Jesus took my sin, paid my penalty and offered me a new life with God.*

*Finally, Robert shared that any person may receive this gift of eternal life by expressing faith in Jesus. He told me of His own conversion years ago and asked me if I believed that Jesus was the Son of God and had died for my sins. I did.*

*For me, it was as if someone had given me the box top picture to a jigsaw puzzle. Previously, I had all the pieces, but never understood how they fit together. Now, hearing the Gospel of Jesus, I was overwhelmed. I finally understood that Jesus had died for me and offered me eternal life!*

*I went home that evening—April 30, 1983—and prayed a simple prayer: "God, I admit that I am a sinner and that my sin has separated me from You. I am sorry for my sin and need Jesus Christ in my life. Thank You for sending your Son to become my substitute. Thank You that Jesus took my sin, died on the cross and rose from the dead to give me new life. I trust in Him alone for my salvation. I ask Him to come into my life and enable me to live the life You always intended for me. In Jesus' name, Amen."*

## AFTER

*That night, nothing supernatural happened that I could see. But, deep in my heart, God began to change me from the inside out. Now that I was adopted as God's son, He began to make me look and live like family. I remember one of the most immediate changes was with my speech. I began to grow disgusted with jokes and comments that I had formerly been entertained by. While I still sinned—and still do—the Holy Spirit began to convict me of unholy habits and give me a longing for God. I began to attend a*

*Christ-exalting church and learned the difference between religion and a deepening relationship with Jesus. And, I am still growing in knowing Him every day since!*

Hopefully, in reading my testimony, you discern several principles. Keep your story simple. Express your need (Before). Make the Gospel clear (How). Clarify sin, the cross and faith. Admit your life isn't perfect, but is progressing (After). Your personal testimony will become one of the most effective tools in your missional toolbox.

## Be Baptized

Jesus' final charge to His disciples was for them to preach the Gospel and baptize believers (Matthew 28:18-20). Because salvation is by grace, baptism cannot be required for salvation. But it is the first, very public declaration of the new Christian's faith in Jesus. The normal practice in the New Testament is that people came to faith and very soon after were baptized. Just as a personal testimony is a verbal witness of the Christian's faith, so baptism is the visible witness. As such, each believer should obey Jesus by being baptized.

There are four powerful symbols associated with baptism that make the practice so important for the Christian. When baptizing converts, pastors will often announce one or more of these symbols to those witnessing the baptism so they may better understand what is happening.

First, your baptism symbolizes cleansing. Hebrews 10:22 encourages us to *"draw near to God with a sincere heart in full assurance of faith, having our hearts sprinkled to cleanse us from a guilty conscience and having our bodies washed with pure water."* Spiritually speaking, the Christian has been purified from sin and stands clean before God. Water baptism doesn't purify a person, but it symbolizes this cleansing.

Second, your baptism symbolizes your resurrection from the dead. In Romans 6:3-5, Paul writes that those *"who were baptized into Christ Jesus were baptized into his death."* That is, having been "buried" with Jesus Christ, the Christian is also "raised with Jesus" to live a brand new life. When the new convert emerges from the water, their baptism symbolizes this resurrection.

Third, your baptism symbolizes surrender. In the act of baptism, new Christians allow themselves to be submerged by someone else. This act of submission symbolizes the surrender each disciple makes to Jesus as Lord. We have been crucified with Christ and we no longer live. Rather, He lives through us (Galatians 2:20).

Fourth, your baptism symbolizes your family unity. Christians come from every culture and express their spiritual life through a variety of denominations and practices. Baptism is one universal practice, shared by all Christians at all times, which symbolizes our family solidarity. 1 Corinthians 12:13 states, *"we were all baptized by one Spirit into one body—whether Jews or Greeks, slave or free—and we were all given the one Spirit to drink."*

Always remember that your baptism doesn't contribute toward your salvation. While it is a deeply significant experience, immersion into water doesn't make a Christian "better." Baptism simply, but beautifully, communicates your cleansing, resurrection, surrender and unity with the whole Body of Christ.

While it is not required, you might consider it helpful to memorialize your baptism with something visible and significant like a note in a journal, a declaration you write and keep, a reminder on the inside cover of your Bible, etc. Sometimes, a Christian may begin to question their own salvation, and this visible reminder may encourage you for a lifetime.

The topic of baptism often raises the question about people who were baptized as infants, or experienced baptism *before* becoming a Christian, perhaps in a moment of pressure or as part of a church or family tradition. As we have learned above, baptism is a *sign* of saving faith. Therefore, it always *follows* an individual's conscious belief in Jesus. A person who was baptized as an infant and later responds to the Gospel should walk in obedience and make a public testimony of their faith through being baptized.

## Be Assured

A prominent theologian observed that there are four kinds of people in every local church:

**1. People who are *not* saved and *know* they are not saved.**
These people are honest in their personal separation from God.

They would unapologetically admit that they are not a Christian and may be disinterested in spiritual things.

### 2. People who are *not* saved but think they *are* saved.

These people have misunderstood the truth of Christianity. They believe they are secure because they were raised in a Christian home, believe God exists, are "good," or attend a particular church. Or, they have followed a non-Christian religion and have been deceived by a lie. These individuals have not believed the true Gospel and will be surprised in eternity.

### 3. People who *are* saved and *know* they are saved.

These people have believed the true Gospel and have confidence in the work of Jesus for them and the promises of Scripture.

### 4. People who *are* saved, but think they are *not* saved.

These people have trusted in Jesus Christ for their salvation, but have not been taught the security of their salvation. So, when they fail, they question whether or not God still loves them.

In 1 John 5:13, the apostle states, *"I write these things to you who believe in the name of the Son of God, so that you may know that you have eternal life."* It is right for Christians to have assurance of their salvation, not because of what they *do*, but because of what Jesus has already *done* for them. Jesus told a parable about seed scattered by a farmer and, in three cases (hardened path, shallow soil and weeds), the seed failed to produce fruit (Matthew 13:1-23). The general warning of the story is that there are all kinds of obstacles that get in the way of fruitful, spiritual growth. Doubt and fear are two of the worst. So, it is crucial for new converts to be confidently rooted in their faith.

Consider these 10 reasons why Christians may be assured of their salvation:

**1. Because of grace.** Ephesians 2:8-9 reminds us, *"For it is by grace you have been saved, through faith—and this not from yourselves, it is the gift of God—not by works, so that no one can boast."* Human performance has no place in salvation (see 2 Timothy 1:9, Romans 11:6). We did nothing to earn our salvation and can do nothing to maintain it. The song

"Amazing Grace" declares, "Grace has brought me safe thus far and grace will lead me home."

**2. Because of justification.** The Westminster Shorter Catechism defines justification as *"an act of God's free grace wherein He pardons all of our sins and accepts us as righteous in his Spirit only for the righteousness of Christ imputed to us and received by faith alone."* This means, because of Jesus' death on the cross, the believer is *legally* declared "not guilty" and is released from all judgment for sin. While Christians still wrestle with sin *conditionally*, we are nonetheless *positionally* righteous and have eternal peace with God (Romans 5:1).

**3. Because of the seal of the Holy Spirit.** Paul announces, *"And you also were included in Christ when you heard the word of truth, the gospel of your salvation. Having believed, you were marked in him with a seal, the promised Holy Spirit, who is a deposit guaranteeing our inheritance until the redemption of those who are God's possession—to the praise of his glory"* (Ephesians 1:13-14). The Holy Spirit living in the believer is a confirmation of our initial salvation and a deposit guaranteeing our final salvation to come. A Christian cannot *not* possess the Spirit, and the residence of the Spirit is evidence of eternal life.

**4. Because of the power of God.** The Christian who fears that they have lost their salvation doesn't understand the infinite power of God to safeguard what He has promised. Jesus said, *"My sheep listen to my voice; I know them, and they follow me. I give them eternal life, and they shall never perish; no one can snatch them out of my hand. My Father, who has given them to me, is greater than all; no one can snatch them out of my Father's hand"* (John 10:27-29). Nothing is able to separate us from God's love (Romans 8:37-39). So we may confidently declare, *"I know whom I have believed, and am convinced that he is able to guard what I have entrusted to him for that day"* (2 Timothy 1:12).

**5. Because of the integrity of God.** What God promises, He ensures. *"God is not a man, that he should lie, nor a son of man, that he should change his mind. Does he speak and then not act? Does he promise and not fulfill?"* (Numbers 23:19). His integrity requires Him to be faithful in everything He has spoken. He never rescinds His gifts (Romans 11:29).

**6. Because we have been changed.** Before faith, every person was spiritually dead. However, once in Christ, a person becomes a "new creation" (2 Corinthians 5:17). They don't merely *act* new; they *are* new. Each Christian possesses an eternally new nature. So, while sometimes believers will not act according to this new nature, we are still "heavenly material." One pastor summarized it this way: "I am not what I should be and I'm not what I will be, but by the grace of God I'm not what I was."

**7. Because we are being changed.** Salvation is both a point-in-time event and a process (more on this in chapter 8). No one becomes completely perfect at the moment of faith. Growth in holiness is a progressive experience that takes a lifetime (2 Corinthians 3:18). So, while all sin is ungodly, it is expected that the Christian will experience success and failure along the way. However, we may have confidence that *"he who began a good work in you will carry it on to completion until the day of Christ Jesus"* (Philippians 1:6).

**8. Because of the intercession of Christ.** Jesus told His disciples that He was "going to prepare a place for" them (John 14:2). This means, in His absence, His children are always on His mind. The Bible teaches that Jesus ascended to the Father and "always lives to intercede" for His people. Because of this heavenly mediation, *"he is able to save completely those who come to God through Him"* (Hebrews 7:25).

**9. Because we have been adopted.** Jesus doesn't just name Christians as His people, but as His family! By faith, we have been declared sons of God (Galatians 3:26), predestined according to the will of God (Ephesians 1:5). Adoption is a legal transaction by a parent to welcome a child into their family with all the rights and privileges of natural born children. Therefore, no child can un-adopt themselves. Our family status is secure, even when we don't act like our Father in heaven.

**10. Because God chose us.** This reason is the coup d'etat of eternal security. Jesus reminds His disciples, *"You did not choose me, but I chose you and appointed you to go and bear fruit"* (John 15:16; see also John 1:12-13). Our salvation is based on a mysterious decision of an all-knowing God who chose us *even though He knew what we would later* *do*! No failure surprises God. He knew all of our deficiencies for all of our life and still chose to give us eternal life.

Surely, any one of these reasons would give confidence to the believer. But all 10 of them together leave no reason for those who are saved not to *know* they are saved, safe and secure in the Father's hand.

## Share the Good News

Just as new mothers love to share their newborn baby, new believers are some of the most effective evangelists because of their enthusiasm about their new life in Jesus. Sharing the Gospel wasn't relegated to an institution, but given as a charge to individuals. Those who have been saved are sent into the world with a saving message to the world in need.

The *message* of the Gospel is addressed earlier in this chapter. There are many helpful *methods* which have proven effective for sharing the Good News. Two are mentioned here.

### One-Verse Evangelism

The Gospel gloriously weaves many verses from the Bible (see the four verses from Romans mentioned under each movement above), but some teachers use Romans 6:23 by itself: *For the wages of sin is death, but the gift of God is eternal life in Christ Jesus our Lord.*

First, on the left side of a piece of paper, write the phrases from the first part of the verse and explain the following ideas (i.e., Write "The wages" and say, "The verse mentions wages which are what a person earns for a work they perform").

| | |
|---|---|
| **The wages** | = What we earn |
| **of sin** | = The reason |
| **is death** | = Eternal destiny |

Next, write the phrases from the second part of the verse on the right side of the paper and explain (i.e., Write "The Gift" and say "A gift is opposite of something we earn. It's freely given").

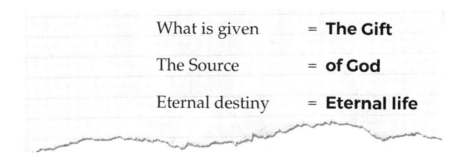

| What is given | = **The Gift** |
|---|---|
| The Source | = **of God** |
| Eternal destiny | = **Eternal life** |

Finally, between the phrases on the left and right side of your page, list the three names/roles of Jesus in the middle. Explain that Jesus is the Messiah promised throughout the Old Testament, that He is the Savior sent from God to rescue humanity and that He is the rightful Lord over our lives.

For the wages of sin is death, but the gift of God is eternal life in Christ Jesus our Lord.

| **The wages** | **CHRIST**<br>(Promised Messiah) | **The Gift** |
|---|---|---|
| **of sin** | **JESUS**<br>(Savior) | **of God** |
| **is death** | **LORD**<br>(God, Master over us) | **Eternal life** |

## Hand-To-Hand Evangelism

Preaching before large crowds, some evangelists have used two chairs to demonstrate our broken relationship with God (turning away) and how God turns to people through His Son, Jesus. The chairs become a visible illustration of a person's connection with God before and after faith in Jesus Christ. In a more personal conversation, you may use your hands effectively. Hold your thumbs out on each hand with your first finger (or all fingers) pointing up to create two "chairs." See Figure 1 on the next page.

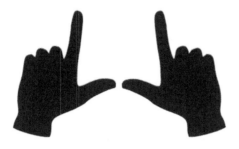

**FIGURE 1**
*The position of our hands reflects people created to be in relationship with God.*

With your hands in this first position, explain that God created human beings for a relationship with Himself. When two people face one another, they are engaged in a conversation or relationship. However, when sin entered the world through Adam, we "turned ourselves away" from God. This turning away is called "sin." All of us are born with this condition and in a position away from God. At this moment, turn your left hand so that your thumb is facing to the left (below). Figure 2 expressed that our "back" is against God, no longer in a relationship.

**FIGURE 2**
*Turn one hand to symbolize that people have turned away from God in rebellion.*

Next, explain that, because God is holy, He cannot tolerate sin and must turn His back on the sinner. Turn your right hand so that your thumb faces the right (Figure 3). Explain that there is now a "chasm" diving human beings and God. Though we try to restore our relationship, there is nothing we can do.

**FIGURE 3**
*In this position, your hands now illustrate the separation people experience between themselves and God because of sin.*

This, of course, is the bad news. And, though we continue to "do right," we cannot become righteous before God on our own. So, God graciously sent His Son into the world to die for sinners. Now it is time to turn your right hand (representing God) back around so that your thumb is facing inward. This illustrates God making a relationship with Himself possible. You may now finish the Gospel presentation by stating that the *only* way we turn toward God is through faith. When we trust in Jesus as our Savior, our relationship with God is restored (turn your left hand back around to the original, starting position).

## SUMMARY

No one begins to walk the spiritual pathway with God until they BELONG to Jesus Christ. Unfortunately, there are many false gospels being offered in our churches and culture. So, we must trust only the right Gospel which is by grace, through faith. Those who believe in Jesus should be baptized and, according to the Scriptures, can have eternal assurance of their salvation. Believers should be able to share the story of what God has done for them personally and be willing to share the Gospel with others around them.

## TAKE THE NEXT STEP

1. Have you personally placed your faith in Jesus alone for your salvation? If not, what is keeping you from trusting in Him? Go back and review the four truths on pages 30-31. You may begin spiritual life with God right now by expressing you faith in the simple prayer on page 32.

2. If you are a Christian, have you been baptized? When did this happen? If you have not been baptized, why? Take the next step by contacting your pastor and scheduling your baptism.

3. Ten reasons were given for why the Christian may be assured of their salvation. Which one is most compelling for you? Why?

4. Why is it important for a Christian to be able to tell their story? If you have not prepared your own testimony using the model presented in this chapter, take some time to do it.

5. What is the most important thing you learned from this chapter?

# BELONG: TO COMMUNITY

*In all but the rarest cases, one is*
*too small a number to produce greatness.*
Warren Bennis

On September 3, 2007, Steve Fossett took off in a single-engine plane from a private airstrip in western Nevada. Several hours later, the record-setting aviator, who was first to fly solo nonstop around the world in a balloon, went missing. Rescuers would eventually search almost 20,000 square miles looking for the downed plane or any sign of Fossett. For a month, two dozen planes flew over the rugged Nevada landscape without success. It wasn't until a year later that a hiker found Fossett's ID card in the mountains and searchers confirmed the crash site.

While no one knows what led to this unfortunate tragedy, one notable failure stands out: Fossett never filed a flight plan. No one knew where he was going, so no one knew where to send help when he was in trouble. The pilot was all alone.

Ecclesiastes 4:8-12 reminds us of the danger of living solo:

*There was a man all alone; he had neither son nor brother. There was no end to his toil, yet his eyes were not content with his wealth.*

| BELONG | | | BECOME | | BEYOND | | |
|--------|--------|--------|--------|--------|--------|--------|--------|
| TO CHRIST | **TO COMMUNITY** | TO CHURCH | INCIDENTAL TRANSFORMATION | INTENTIONAL TRANSFORMATION | INTO MY CHURCH | INTO MY NEIGHBORHOOD | INTO MY WORLD |

*"For whom am I toiling," he asked, "and why am I depriving my-self of enjoyment?" This too is meaningless— a miserable business! Two are better than one, because they have a good return for their work: If one falls down, his friend can help him up. But pity the man who falls and has no one to help him up! Also, if two lie down together, they will keep warm. But how can one keep warm alone? Though one may be overpowered, two can defend themselves. A cord of three strands is not quickly broken.*

God never intended people to live in isolation, but to live in community. After declaring all of creation "good," God said, "It is *not* good for man to be alone" (Genesis 2:18) and made a suitable partner for Adam who would share in his work, be a friend to lift him up, help keep him warm and share in his struggle. Two were better than one in the Garden of Eden. Two has been better since that time. The biblical community expressed in the first family is a pattern of the biblical community intended in the family of God, the church, today. Once a person BELONGS to Jesus Christ, we want to help them BELONG to community, enjoying the benefits of life together so that they do not fly solo in their spiritual life.

Biblical community may be described many different ways. One ministry leader defines it as "The people of God doing the work of God together." Another leader states, "People in relationship to Jesus Christ and one another who are living the Christian life together as partners with God in His mission." No matter *how* people define community, the Bible clearly underlines the importance of it.

The first biblical community is modeled in Acts 2. It is significant that Peter preached a gospel sermon and the church grew to 3000 people in one day (vv. 1-41). Later, Peter miraculously healed an invalid who began to walk and the news spread throughout the region. The church was making a great impact outwardly. But, what was happening *inwardly* was the fuel for their ministry. Notice Acts 2:42-47,

*They devoted themselves to the apostles' teaching and to fellowship, to the breaking of bread and to prayer. Everyone was filled with awe at the many wonders and signs performed by the apos-*

*tles. All the believers were together and had everything in com-*
*mon. They sold property and possessions to give to anyone who*
*had need. Every day they continued to meet together in the temple*
*courts. They broke bread in their homes and ate together with glad*
*and sincere hearts, praising God and enjoying the favor of all the*
*people. And the Lord added to their number daily those who were*
*being saved.*

Though the Apostle Peter was in the spotlight as preacher and
miracle worker, he was part of a collective community. It was *all* the
Christians frequently meeting together to grow, learn, pray, worship
and give together that made Peter and others so effective. It was in
biblical community that Peter was developed and strengthened and
gained vision for the work Jesus called him to do.

This is the common model found throughout the Bible. Effective
ministers are supported by supportive communities. Moses was
helped by Aaron, Hur, Joshua and Caleb. King David was surrounded by a corps of "mighty men" (2 Samuel 23:8-39). In the book of Ne-
hemiah, the people of God rebuilt the wall of Jerusalem by standing
side by side with other families. Jesus sent His disciples out in pairs,
not alone, to do the work of ministry (Luke 10:1). Even the capable
Apostle Paul lists dozens of people he calls "dear friends," "fellow
workers" and "family" in Romans 16. In his book *Organizing Genius*,
author Warren Bennis writes,

> We cling to the myth of the Lone Ranger, the romantic idea that
> great things are usually accomplished by a larger-than-life indi-
> vidual working alone...But, in a global society...collaboration is
> not simply desirable, it is inevitable. In all but the rarest cases,
> one is too small a number to produce greatness. (p. 2)

God accomplishes His purposes through individuals. But, usual-
ly, such individuals are surrounded by a vital, biblical community.
Your health, as a Christian will, in part, be based on your healthy
connection to community. As we can see from Acts 2:42-47 mentioned above, there are several personal and spiritual benefits of community:

## COMMUNITY PRINCIPLE #1

*In Community, We Hear and See Truth Taught and Proved*

As Luke records the first Christians meeting together, he states, "they devoted themselves to the apostles' teaching" (v. 42). We should remember that "they" refers to the newly converted crowd of 3000 (see v. 41). None of them had walked with Jesus during the previous three years. They had not heard His teachings firsthand. They likely understood very little about the crucifixion and resurrection. The church at this time was a group of immature Christians who were just beginning their spiritual journey.

So, on regular occasion they came together to listen, learn, think and talk about spiritual truth. Not only did they grow under the apostles' teaching, they also had opportunity to observe new spiritual ideas being lived out through others in the community.

When Christians gather with other Christians, they can talk about God's Word in a way that fits their reality. In other words, they get to discuss how truth works in *their* world, not just *the* world. Rather than just hear lofty principles preached on Sunday, they get to discover how spiritual truth applies to their specific life circumstances. Not only that, they get to witness those truths at work in the lives of others as they *"observe one another's conduct"* (2 Timothy 3:10).

I have learned about generosity by hearing how my friends have demonstrated rich generosity. I have become a better parent by watching how godly adults in my community parent their children. I have learned how to *"consider others more important than yourselves"* (Philippians 2:3) by observing my spiritual mentor take extra time in conversation with someone in need. I could have heard a sermon, read a book or attended a conference addressing these life skills. But, when I hear and see truth taught and proved among "my people," it inspires me to live the same way.

## COMMUNITY PRINCIPLE #2

*In Community, We Discover the Blessing of Give and Take*

Verse 42 adds that the Christians "devoted themselves to the fellowship." Though the description of the first Christian community describes eating and meeting together, the Greek word *koinonia* means much more. The word means "to share." And the early disciples experienced sharing in a radical way.

Luke writes, *"All the believers were together and had everything in common..."* (vv. 44-45). According to the needs of the group, some would share what they owned in order to supply the needs of others. Chapter 4 gives a specific example. A disciple named Joseph sold a piece of property and gave the money to the apostles to be distributed among other members who had little. Not surprisingly, the community gave Joseph the nickname Barnabas, which translates "son of encouragement" (Acts 4:36-37), because he encouraged so many through his generosity.

Even Paul wasn't above receiving help from others. He thanked the Christians in Philippi for being partners in the Gospel with him (Philippians 1:3) and sharing in his troubles (4:14). When he wrote to the Christians in Rome, he said, *"I pray that now at last by God's will the way may be opened for me to come to you. I long to see you so that I may impart to you some spiritual gift to make you strong—that is, that you and I may be mutually encouraged by each other's faith"* (Romans 1:10-12). Paul hoped to strengthen the young Christians, but he also hoped to be encouraged by them. Give and take.

At Pantego Bible Church, we have been fortunate enough to see and experience this blessing of give and take at work in biblical communities throughout our congregation. Christians support one another when one falls ill and needs others to prepare meals or take care of everyday tasks. Christians have finished home repairs for a brother who was suddenly unemployed. Others helped a family in their community move across town. In my own community, other adults have been trusted counselors for our children in life decisions. Sometimes, the blessing is less tangible such as emotional and spiritual support or the strong faith of one member encouraging another to endure hardship. We have prayed with one another, grieved with one another, celebrated with one another and challenged one another (Hebrews 10:24-25). Sometimes we offer a blessing, sometimes we receive one.

This mutual sharing makes a church stronger. On the one hand, members grow to unselfishly give themselves to others. On the other hand, each member becomes vulnerable enough to express their need and receive loving assistance. This give and take helps the church grow from mere acquaintances to deep and abiding relationships.

I once heard a fable that illustrated this blessing. A man spoke with the Lord about heaven and hell. "I will show you Hell," said the Lord. And they went into a room which had a large pot of stew in the middle. The smell was delicious and around the pot sat people who were famished and desperate. All were holding spoons with very long handles which reached to the pot, but because the handles of the spoons were longer than their arms, it was impossible to get the stew into their mouths. Their suffering was terrible.

"Now I will show you Heaven," said the Lord, and they went into an identical room. There was a similar pot of stew and the people had the same identical spoons, but they were well nourished, talking and happy. At first the man did not understand. "It is simple," said the Lord. "You see, as family, they have learned to feed each other."

This is the uniqueness of biblical community.

## COMMUNITY PRINCIPLE #3
### *In Community, We Experience the Joy of Authentic Spiritual Relationships*

In his book *True Spirituality: Becoming a Romans 12 Christian*, author and pastor Chip Ingram comments on research conducted by Robert Putnam in 2000 where he declared that "loneliness is America's new epidemic." Ingram adds,

> *Belonging is a God-given human need. We all need and want the security of belonging to a family, belonging to a group, belonging to a team, belonging with people who need us just like we need them in a healthy and productive way. The fragmentation of the family and the rapid growth in technology have made people more mobile and isolated than ever before. The aching need to belong is at an all-time high.*

The early Christians belonged to each other, because they first belonged to Christ. They met together, dined together, worshipped together and enjoyed being with each other frequently. Their relationships were described as "sincere." The word literally translates as "simple" or "single-minded." That is, their friendships were genuine, real, and authentic. Those who were formerly strangers became the best of friends.

This is different than having "church friends," as my colleague, Dr. Tom Bulick explains. A person can attend church and have a handful of people they see at church every week and associate with around church Bible studies, worship services or meetings. But, outside of church, they have no other contact with these church friends. Biblical community consists of more than those casual, weekly acquaintances. Community is the gathering of friends who you count on. They are the people you call when you are in need, the people you wish to invite to dinner and the ones you would want at your bedside in the hospital.

A year into my pastoral ministry at Pantego Bible Church, I witnessed the power of authentic relationships. The son of a prominent leader in our church was involved in a tragic automobile accident. As he was rushed into surgery, word spread throughout the family's community. Within an hour, the hospital waiting room was flooded with dozens of people who came to support their friends. Over the next few days and weeks, as the young man endured additional surgeries, the amputation of one leg and a difficult recovery, the waiting room stayed full. There was never a time when community was *not* present to pray, support and help.

On one of my trips to the hospital to visit with the family, I was introduced to a lady whose husband was the victim of a shooting and was near death. She told me that she was a Christian and, in fact, used to attend our church many years ago. However, she and her family left the church and never connected in community with other Christians after that time. She had no spiritual friends who would walk with her through this most traumatic time in her life.

At that hospital, the contrast between living in community and living alone was startling. On one side of the waiting room were emotional support, prayers, meals, and acts of kindness from true friends. On the other side was a Christian who had no one on whom she could depend. It was a reminder to me that authentic, lifelong relationships are forged in community.

## COMMUNITY PRINCIPLE #4
*In Community, We Demonstrate the Power of the Gospel*

Luke notes that, as the early Christians met together, they enjoyed the favor of outsiders and the Lord *"added to their number daily those who were being saved"* (v. 47). Michael Green, in his book *Evangelism in the Early Church,* observes that the remarkable way in which Christians loved each other and their neighbors affirmed the transformative power of the Gospel.

> *They made the grace of God credible by a society of love and mutual care which astonished pagans and was recognized as something entirely new. It lent persuasiveness to the claim that the new age had dawned in those who were giving it flesh. The message of the kingdom became more than an idea. A new human community had sprung up and looked very much like the new order to which the evangelist had pointed. Here love was given daily expression; reconciliation was actually occurring; people were no longer divided into Jews and Gentiles, slave and free, male and female. In this community the weak were protected, the stranger welcomed. People were healed; the poor and dispossessed were cared for and found justice. Almost everything was shared. Joy abounded and ordinary lives were filled with praise.*

Biblical communities model unconditional love, sacrifice, mutual concern, kindness, impartiality, generosity, faith and blessing—all virtues rooted in the Gospel of Jesus. As the world looks on, outsiders will "know we are Christians by our love for one another" (John 13:35) and will catch a glimpse of Christ's love for them, through us.

## What Makes Community Biblical

An after-school chess club or a local choir might qualify as community. A group of neighborhood mothers who meet weekly to share cares and concerns could be called a community. Young adults promoting safer environmental changes could be a community. Communities are people sharing a common place with a common purpose.

For this reason, *biblical* community is so significant. Christians who gather in community are not just *any* people, but the chosen people of God—*His* people. And, our purpose in gathering together is to *"declare the praises of Him who called us out of darkness and into His wonderful light"* (1 Peter 2:9). Biblical community isn't a social group, a dinner party or a Bible study, though it may include those things. Biblical community is a particular people who belong to God and each other for a particular purpose.

At Pantego Bible Church, we highlight 7 Functions of Biblical Community.* These are the regular expressions of God's people living on purpose. Some of these functions are inward, directing the group's attention to one another. Other functions are outward, directing the group's attention to those not in their group. We talk about facing our chairs inward to one another and outward to others.

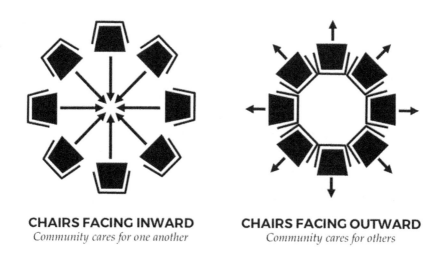

**CHAIRS FACING INWARD**
*Community cares for one another*

**CHAIRS FACING OUTWARD**
*Community cares for others*

Biblical communities must have both kinds of experiences. If they always "face inward," they will become self-centered, closed and insensitive to the needs of the world around them. If they always "face

*These 7 Functions of Biblical Community were first introduced to Pantego Bible Church by pastor Randy Frazee in 2000. For more information about biblical community, the importance of community for Christian growth or these various functions of community, see Frazee's *The Connecting Church*, 2009, HarperCollins.

outward," they will neglect the personal needs of the group and eventually become less effective in fulfilling their purpose. The following explains the 7 Functions of Biblical Community with practical examples of how these functions have worked out in various biblical communities.

## Inward Functions

**Spiritual Formation**—Almost everything a group does together has a spiritually formative benefit. However, each community should intentionally devote their attention to activities or disciplines which encourage spiritual growth. This includes Bible study, prayer, worship and the Lord's Table. This special time encourages spiritual reflection, remembrance and rejoicing in who God is and what He has done.

In the small group community my wife and I attend (called a "home group"), we pray every time we are together and study the Bible or a Christian book about every other week together. Other groups have met for an evening of worship or fasted together.

**Recreation**—When the early church came together, they ate together with "glad and sincere hearts." This means they enjoyed being together. Biblical communities are not always serious. They play together, enjoying recreational activities together. This may be as simple as communities eating together when they gather. Deeper friendships are also built through playing games, celebrating family milestones or traveling together.

Most communities in our church share a meal together almost every week and often attend sports games, run/walk races or attend children's school events together. Some families have taken vacations together. I know one community that hosts an annual soup contest where each family brings their favorite recipe and everyone enjoys tasting and voting on their favorite.

**Care**—In too many churches, people expect their pastor to visit the sick, encourage the hopeless, comfort the suffering or pursue the sinner who wanders away. While it is important for pastors to demonstrate care for their people, the New Testament model shows biblical communities, not just pastors, caring for one another. To be certain, those who have the closest relationship to an individual can offer the most meaningful care. So, biblical communities see themselves as the church given to each other to meet one another's needs.

Most communities take meals to member families who are in crisis and visit one another in the hospital. They run errands for one another, watch each other's children and help with home maintenance for those who are unable. In one instance, a community planned and put together a wedding for one of its members who was unable to afford the event.

## Outward Functions

**Serving/Volunteering**—Healthy biblical communities serve and support their church. Because they *are* the church, they help their church fulfill its mission. They don't all have to serve in the same ministry together at the same time (though some communities find great satisfaction in doing so), but they challenge each other to use their spiritual gifts to "build up the body."

Communities have served our church's children's ministry, all together on a specific Sunday of the month. At a large Easter festival hosted by our church, my home group served together cooking food for our neighbors. The men in one community serve together to do landscaping for the church.

**Evangelism**—Very often, evangelism is thought of as an individual responsibility or a church "program." But, so much evangelism in the early church was accomplished through communities—people sharing the Gospel together, or evangelists being supported by a specific community in their work. Biblical communities participate in the whole work of evangelism by praying for unbelievers, inviting unbelievers into their group to experience biblical love and acceptance, encouraging one another to share their faith and supporting the ministry of evangelism in their church.

My community encourages each other to share the Gospel in their own areas of influence. We pray for unbelievers and have hosted holiday "block parties" to gather our unchurched neighbors together to hear the Gospel. In one instance, several women in our community prepared desserts for another member who was hosting an open house and discussion about Jesus for her neighbors.

Even in the strategic work of door-to-door evangelism, biblical community is essential. Jesus sent His disciples in pairs to share the Gospel. Two or more Christians can support each other in the evangelistic task, pray for the one who is sharing and be a witness of mutual love and respect to the watching world.

**Local Compassion**—Biblical communities are aware of the needs in their local neighborhood or town and work together to extend compassion outside their church. They seek justice for the marginalized, defend the helpless, support the homeless, feed the hungry and clothe the poor. Through each act of service, those who are far from God experience the benefits of the Kingdom through God's people.

There are so many ways that communities can make a difference in their world. My community makes 100 sack lunches for a local homeless shelter several times a year. We have worked together on maintenance projects at another local church. Some groups raise money to provide school supplies to needy children each year. One group has sorted food together at a food pantry. Another collected money to help a family in their neighborhood who lost their house to fire. Each of these are real expressions of compassion.

**International Mission**—Communities "face their chairs outward" not only by living on mission locally, but also globally. International missions is the task of the church and the church is made up of smaller communities. Therefore, communities must ever be "on mission," growing a heart for the nations. Sometimes, this means members *go* on mission together and at other times, it means they *support* mission together.

While the mission field seems so far away, there are a number of simple ways communities can be involved in international missions. They can financially support one or more of their members who dare to travel to a mission field. Or, they may invite a visiting missionary to their meeting to talk about their particular ministry. Groups can pray for unreached people groups in the world, attend a mission conference together or read and discuss a book about world missions.

Regularly practicing these 7 Functions of Biblical Community causes a group to grow deeper with one another and have a greater impact in their world. In addition, its members experience a variety of transformational experiences that holistically impact their hearts, minds, hands and feet.

## SUMMARY

This chapter highlights the next step in the spiritual pathway: Belonging to community. God has designed us for relationships with Him and with one another. Two are better than one. Therefore, Christians must not neglect the habit of meeting with each other. Once in community, members practice inward and outward functions, "facing their chairs inward" in ministry to one another and "facing their chairs outward" in ministry to those outside the group. The 7 Functions of Biblical Community include spiritual formation, recreation, care, serving/volunteering together, evangelism, local compassion and international mission.

## TAKE THE NEXT STEP

1. Most spiritual transformation happens in community. Who has had the most significant impact on your life? What does this teach you about the value of community?

2. Are you presently connected in community at your church? If not, what obstacles prevent you from taking this step? Prayerfully and courageously take this step by finding out more about biblical community in your church.

3. Which of the four Community Principles is most valuable to you? Why?

4. Which of the three Inward Functions—spiritual formation, recreation and care—is most difficult for you? What do you need to do to better practice this function in your own community?

5. Which of the four Outward Functions—serving, evangelism, local compassion and international mission—is most difficult for you? What do you need to do to better practice this function in your own community?

6. What is the most important thing you learned from this chapter?

# BELONG: TO CHURCH

*The church exists for nothing else*
*but to draw men into Christ.*
C.S. Lewis

In the last chapter, we considered the importance of Christians belonging to biblical community—a group of other believers with whom they may do life together. According to Scripture, this gathering is an expression of the church. But, belonging to community is not the same thing as belonging to a local church, the "family of believers" (Galatians 6:10). In this chapter, we will consider the importance of taking this step on the spiritual pathway.

Before we explore how to BELONG to church, we must lay a theological foundation of the church. Though we speak of "going to church," Christ's church isn't a building or a location per se. The word for church in the New Testament, *ekklesia*, means "those called" or "an assembly." In chapter 1, we identified the initial call to faith. The church is the corporate assembly of all those who have been "called to belong to Jesus" (Romans 1:6).

In light of this, the church is universal and local. That is, the church of Jesus is the unity of believers all over the world at one time

| BELONG | | | BECOME | | BEYOND | | |
|---|---|---|---|---|---|---|---|
| TO CHRIST | TO COMMUNITY | **TO CHURCH** | INCIDENTAL TRANSFORMATION | INTENTIONAL TRANSFORMATION | INTO MY CHURCH | INTO MY NEIGHBORHOOD | INTO MY WORLD |

manifesting itself in many local expressions. The church is also visible and invisible. In other words, we can see the church each week as Christians gather together in worship and learning. But, what we can see with our eyes isn't the totality of the church. The Lord knows who are His (2 Timothy 2:19) and there may be some unseen Christians, perhaps not connected to a local church, who are still part of Christ's church.

People BELONG to the church at conversion. Paul writes in 1 Corinthians 12:13, *"For we were all baptized by one Spirit into one body—whether Jews or Greeks, slave or free—and we were all given the one Spirit to drink."* All Christians were immersed (baptized) by the Spirit into the spiritual Body of Christ. The residence of the Holy Spirit in each believer unites them with all other believers throughout time. The Spirit is our common bond.

Before moving on, it is helpful to summarize these important distinctives and give an example of each:

**Local Church**—Churches meeting at a particular address in a location are referred to as local churches. Larger cities may have dozens of local churches represented by a variety of denominations. In the illustration below, the region has four local churches.

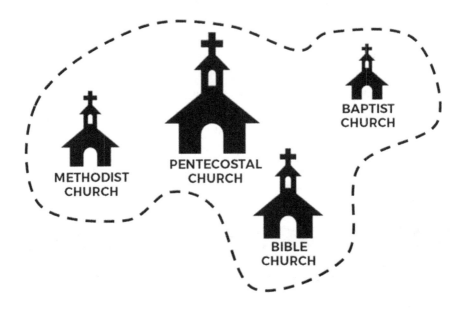

**Visible Church**—This is the church as *we* see it. It's the physical location and all the people who gather there at any time. The visible, local church is made of all kinds of people—mature Christians, new Christians, unbelievers, seekers, doubters, etc. Though "the Lord knows who are His" (2 Timothy 2:19), it is impossible for us to know the spiritual condition of any person in the visible church at any time.

**Universal Church**—This group is comprised of all Christians in all places, no matter what church they attend. In some rare instances, Christians don't attend a local church. Still, they are regarded as a part of the universal Body of Christ. Just as a physical family is united by "blood ties," so the family of God, no matter where each person lives, is united by the "blood tie" of Jesus Christ. In Christ, we all form one body (Romans 12:5) in which *"There is neither Jew nor Greek, slave nor free, male nor female, for you are all one in Christ Jesus"* (Galatians 3:28).

The relationship between the local church and the universal church may be represented by the illustration below:

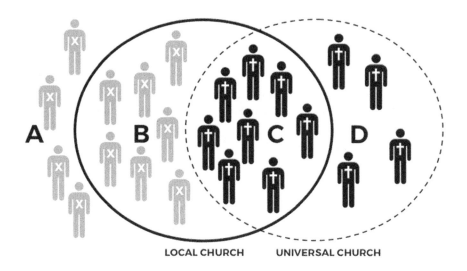

LOCAL CHURCH    UNIVERSAL CHURCH

Some people, represented by people in area A, are non-Christians outside the universal church and do not attend any local church. This is the harvest field each church is called to cultivate.

Other people, represented by people in area B, attend a local, visible church but are not part of the universal church. That is, they are unbelievers who attend church because of tradition, invitation or a misunderstanding of what it means to be a Christ-follower. Author A.W. Tozer comments, *"One hundred religious persons knit into a unity by careful organization do not constitute a church any more than eleven dead men make a [sports] team. The first requirement is life, always."*

Some people, represented by people in area D, are part of the universal church but don't attend any local church. This means there are Christians who have not yet connected in a church where they live. Perhaps they are new to the area. Or, they may have stopped going to church because of conflict or disappointment with leadership. In ministry circles, we sometimes refer to these people, not as *un*-churched, but as *de*-churched people. They have disconnected from God's people, but this doesn't mean they have disconnected from God.

Still other people, represented by the people in area C, are genuine Christians who are part of the true, universal church *and* regularly attend a local church. These believers are those who BELONG to Christ and BELONG to a church at some level. This is our goal for all people. We want to help people take this step along the spiritual pathway.

A few examples will help us understand the distinctions between the visible church, the local church and the universal church.

Marcos lives in a small town in Texas. His family attends one of three local churches in his town. Marcos has attended with his family since he was a child. However, Marcos has never personally put his faith in Jesus Christ. Marcos is not a Christian. We would say that Marcos is a part of the local, visible church, but he is not in the universal church of Jesus Christ.

Sara was listening to a radio program where an evangelist clearly explained the reality of sin and the sacrifice of Jesus Christ. As the preacher prayed, Sara also prayed and received Jesus into her life. Unsure of what steps to take, Sara did not immediately begin attending a church in her city. So, we would say that Sara is not part of the local, visible church but she *is* a member of the universal church because of her faith in Jesus.

When Kevin moved to Atlanta for business, he met Joseph, another Christian. Both men attended different churches on the week-end. Kevin chose to attend a church with a few of his business but learned, in time, that neither of his partners were Christians, though they attended church regularly. In this example, we would say that Kevin and Joseph attend two different local churches. The visible church Kevin attends includes him and his business colleagues even though not all of them are Christian. Only Kevin and Joseph (not the business partners) are members of the universal church—a unity transcending all tribal, ethnic, cultural and denominational distinctions because it is rooted in Jesus Christ.

Margaret was arrested for narcotics possession and was sent to jail for 5 years. While there, a prison chaplain visited her, gave Margaret a Bible and introduced her to Jesus. After her conversion, Margaret begin attending a prison Bible study, but was unable to attend any local church. So, we would say that Margaret isn't in the local church, but *is* a member of the universal church.

The reason for these distinctions is not to create unfair judgments about people. Rather, they help Christians understand the nature of "the church." We should never assume that everyone in our church is at the same place in their spiritual journey. Your church is filled with Christians and non-Christians. As well, knowing that Christians fill many different types of churches and some may not even yet be attending a church, protects us from assumptions about others and cultivates a spirit of charity among people who might practice their faith differently than we do.

## Membership in the Local Church

The New Testament church didn't know anything of official church membership because all those who gathered together *were* Christians. Persecution among the earliest followers of Jesus meant that the church gathered at great personal risk to each of its members. So, there was no need to distinguish between those who were truly part of the Body of Christ and those who weren't. Today, however, we must realize that the church is a mixed group of people and membership is the means by which church leaders may discern which attendees have the capacity for spiritual maturity and may be held accountable for their new life in Jesus Christ.

Because there is no biblical model of church membership, each church may design a process that fits its goals. At Pantego Bible Church, we have three elements in our membership process: a membership class, a membership interview and a membership covenant.

A membership class is offered to membership candidates to teach them the core doctrine of the church, share the true Gospel of Jesus and highlight membership expectations. It is not uncommon for attendees who *think* they are Christians to learn that they have not believed the truth and come to a knowledge of the truth through this class. Member expectations (discussed below) and a description of the spiritual pathway enable candidates to understand what they are committing to.

Following the membership class, each candidate is subject to a membership interview. Conducted by pastors, elders, deacons or other official church leadership, this brief interview affords candidates an opportunity to share their personal testimony. In this way, church leadership attempt to verify the genuineness of each member's faith. Additionally, leadership may use the interview to match each candidate's spiritual gift(s) with ministry opportunities in the church. And, this is a great occasion for the new member to be introduced to biblical community so they may connect with others.

This doesn't conclude a person's membership in the church; it initiates the new member into a new level of "belonging" in the local church. We present each candidate with a membership covenant which encourages the new member to fulfill their responsibility to Christ's church. This responsibility includes unity, community, ministry, generosity, authority and accountability. Each of these shall be discussed in turn.

## UNITY

The psalmist declares the joy of unity among God's people, *"How good and pleasant it is when God's people live together in unity"* (Psalm 133:1). Jesus prayed that His disciples would be *"brought to complete unity"* (John 17:23). And Paul urged Christians to *"Make every effort to keep the unity of the Spirit through the bond of peace"* (Ephesians 4:3).

Unity is important among God's people because unity is a virtue shared by the Father, the Son and the Holy Spirit who exist in perfect harmony (Deuteronomy 6:4; John 17:11). When Christians live in unity, they reflect the unity of the godhead. For this reason, Paul describes the church as one "body" which contains many and various "parts" (1 Corinthians 12). Each of the parts, or members, is essential for the operation of the whole body, the church. No part is greater than the others. No part is dispensable. In his book *Simply Christian: Why Christianity Makes Sense,* theologian N.T. Wright describes church unity like a river:

> [T]hough the church consists by definition of people from the "widest possible variety of backgrounds, part of the point of it all is that they belong to one another, and are meant to be part of the same powerful flow, going now in the same single direction. Diversity gives way to unity." (p. 200)

The expression of this important unity isn't found simply in gathering together at the same place at the same time each week. Just because Christians are members of the same church doesn't necessarily mean that they are living together in unity. There are several telling indicators of true unity.

**Those who love unity affirm diversity.** They embrace the differences between people and appreciate social, educational, economic, ethnic and racial differences. Churches and members committed to unity don't discriminate. While each owns their own preferences, they can affirm a variety of styles, methods or opinions. This means that leaders and members are gracious in tolerating different theological positions on matters that are considered "non-essential" to life and faith. Because Jesus' church is made up of people from every nation, tribe and tongue (Revelation 7:9), those in the church should expect the church to be filled with many cultural, national and personal expressions. Therefore, its members affirm diversity.

**Those who love unity accept change**. Every healthy, living organism changes over time. Yet some people in the church have great difficulty with change—changing worship styles, changing leadership, changing schedules, changing traditions, changing ministry direction. Intolerance to change often leads to conflict which, in turn, divides the church. Members who endure change set aside their preferences for the sake of the greater good. They look out not only for their own interests, but also for the interests of others (Philippians 2:4). They don't grumble or gossip, but accept change for the sake of unity.

**Those who love unity address conflict.** The unwillingness to be reconciled with others leads to the fracturing of families, marriages, communities and the church. Too often, rather than confront, apologize, forgive and restore, Christians—who have been reconciled to God—refuse to be reconciled to one another. This "root of bitterness" begins to grow and causes trouble among individuals and the greater church (Hebrews 12:15).

Children of God should resolve conflict in the family of God. This means that members resist judging one another (Matthew 7:1), forgive "as they have been forgiven" (Ephesians 4:32), confess their sins to one another (James 5:16) and be agents of reconciliation in their church (2 Corinthians 5:18). As we shall see later, this *doesn't* mean that Christians should excuse sin against one another, but they should always look for a way of restoration. Only when conflict is identified and reconciled is unity preserved.

**Those who love unity advance together.** They embrace a common vision and head in the same direction *as one*. Amos 3:3 asks, *"Do two walk together unless they have agreed to do so?"* The answer is, "Of course not!" No two people walk together, in a common direction, unless they have mutual agreement. When people become church members, they are agreeing to walk in the direction the church and its leadership are going. There is no place for renegade members— attendees pushing their own agendas, promoting initiatives not in line with their church. A church cannot afford for its members to embrace two-thirds of its mission. Membership means all the people, going all the way to accomplish all the mission that God has given them.

Many years ago, a longtime attendee of our church stopped into my office to mention a concern. He didn't much appreciate the style of music that we presented in our worship services and preferred that we sing more classic hymns. I appreciated his willingness to talk with me personally and explained the strategic reason why we offered the style of worship we did. His humble response was remarkable, "Pastor, I wish I could have *my* way. But *either* way, I will be here every Sunday because this is my church!" I was so grateful that he valued us moving our mission together rather than him getting his way. That's unity!

## COMMUNITY

As Paul describes the church in 1 Corinthians 12, he commands, *"there should be no division in the body, but its parts should have equal concern for each other. If one part suffers, every part suffers with it; if one part is honored, every part rejoices with it"* (vv. 25-26). The phrase "equal concern" means "anxiety of care for others." This is a good test of authentic church membership: A person genuinely cares for others.

In my 25 years of being a pastor, I've heard a handful of people say, "I don't really need church." While everyone needs connection with others, the statement proves a misunderstanding of being part of the church. Church is not a consumer experience where we only think about what we *get* out of it. Church is a community of people who *give* themselves to one another. Church members are committed to community—supporting, loving, protecting, challenging, encouraging, confronting and serving one another. Church members connect in community.

## MINISTRY

Church members not only give themselves to one another in community, they also give themselves to their church in ministry. Each Christian is given a *"manifestation of the Spirit...for the common good"* (1 Corinthians 12:7). This means God has gifted each believer to bless others.

For this reason, the term "membership" can be misleading. A person can be a member of a club, organization or association and never participate in anything. I have a friend who is a member of a health club but never goes. A person can hold a membership to a museum and never contribute anything. They might visit occasionally to look at the artwork, but aren't likely to help with the landscaping or sweep the floors. Membership may be a very passive experience.

When we speak of membership in the local church, we really mean *partnership*, which implies cooperation, mutual effort and working together toward a common goal. Business partners share all of the sacrifice and enjoy all the benefits. Partners in rock climbing take responsibility for the safety and success of each other.

The Apostle Paul thanked the Philippian Christians for their partnership: *"I thank my God every time I remember you. In all my prayers for all of you, I always pray with joy because of your partnership in the gospel from the first day until now"* (Philippians 1:3-5). While Paul served the church, those in the church reciprocated in their ministry to Paul. The word "partnership" means "to share." It's the same word Paul uses in 2 Corinthians 8:3-4, *"For I testify that they gave as much as they were able, and even beyond their ability. Entirely on their own, they urgently pleaded with us for the privilege of sharing in this service to the Lord's people."* The Corinthian Christians eagerly desired to share themselves— to partner with Paul in his service to others. We will talk more about the believer's ministry in chapter 10.

## GENEROSITY

Perhaps more difficult than giving our time in ministry is giving our money for ministry. But giving is a defining practice for disciples of Jesus. There are more than 800 references to money in the Bible, and Jesus spoke about money more than He taught about heaven or hell. Our Savior taught that how a believer uses his money proves what matters most to him. *"For where your treasure is, there your heart will be also"* (Matthew 6:21).

I have a series of three sermons on giving that I preach to my church every few years. I teach that the way a Christian gives or withholds their financial resources says much about their spiritual life. I explain that money is the "currency of Kingdom citizenship." From Jesus' Parable of the Rich Ruler (Luke 18:18-30), we see that Kingdom people surrender to Jesus their King, trust in Jesus their King and delight in Jesus their King. Their giving is proof of their citizenship.

In the second sermon, I teach that money is the "currency of God-centered worship." Jesus' Parable of the Talents (Luke 19:11-27) is the story of a master who entrusts His resources to his servants to use in such a way that it produces a profit. While some parables are more difficult to interpret, this one is simple: God has entrusted His resources to His people to use in His absence in such a way as to make much of God. Generosity results when Christians remember that God is the original owner of everything, that they have a responsibility to manage what God gives and that what we do with God's resources proves what we think about God.

In the final sermon, I communicate that money is the "currency of extraordinary faith." From the beautiful story of the widow who gave her two meager coins in the temple (Luke 21:1-4), I teach about the importance of faith in the spiritual life. Hebrews 11:6 reminds us, *"And without faith it is impossible to please God, because anyone who comes to him must believe that he exists and that he rewards those who earnestly seek him."* What we give, how much we give and why we give is an opportunity to express our faith in God who provides everything for our lives.

Having established this biblical foundation, I don't apologize for urging God's people to give because I believe that generosity is a chance for people to grow deeper in their relationship with God. And, because each member embraces the mission of their church and wishes to advance that mission, their giving is their opportunity to participate in what God is doing. For this reason, we teach that members of the church give. They express biblical generosity.

## AUTHORITY

Those who belong to their church submit to the leadership of their church. Just as many people want to be followers of Christ without surrendering to his lordship, so many people want to belong to a church without submitting to leadership. But no organization succeeds without established leaders and willing followers.

Submission isn't just helpful; it's biblical. Paul commands, *"Everyone must submit himself to the governing authorities, for there is no authority except that which God has established. The authorities that exist have been established by God"* (Romans 13:1). Likewise, Peter commands, *"Submit yourselves for the Lord's sake to every authority instituted among men: whether to the king, as the supreme authority, or to governors, who are sent by him to punish those who do wrong and to commend those who do right"* (1 Peter 2:13-14). It's important to remember that these commands were written to Christians who were under the authority of rulers who were not Christians. So, the command to submit wasn't conditioned on authorities who were godly. Submission to authority is a noble virtue.

This is where Satan faltered. He attempted to subvert the rightful, supreme authority of God and assert his own will (see Genesis 3:1-5 and Isaiah 14:12-15). This autonomy, or "self-rule," was rebellion that attempted to exalt himself and dethrone God. The result was corruption of all of creation.

When God's people reject the God-given authority of leaders in the church, they corrupt the church. They cause conflict. They create division. They present a poor witness of the church. And they prevent the church from achieving its mission. For this reason, church members must respect authority.

## ACCOUNTABILITY

So far, we have considered five important expectations of church members: unity, community, ministry, generosity and authority. Occasionally, those in the church don't live up to these expectations. This is where accountability comes in. Unlike those who attend a church without the commitment of membership, those who are members welcome accountability in their spiritual lives.

Accountability is "the willingness to accept responsibility" and requires two parties. On the one hand, church members must be willing to be held accountable. That is, they invite spiritual scrutiny of their speech, character and behavior by trusted friends. The psalmist prayed, *"Search me, O God, and know my heart; test me and know my anxious thoughts. See if there is any offensive way in me, and lead me in the way everlasting"* (Psalm 139:23-24). All Christians should be open for God to "search them," inwardly by His Holy Spirit and outwardly by the gentle confrontation of others. What made King David—an adulterer, liar and murderer—a "man after God's own heart" is not that he never sinned, but that he was willing to be held accountable by the prophet Nathan (see 2 Samuel 12:1-13).

On the other hand, members must care enough about others in the church that they will humbly confront those who are not walking in a manner worthy of Christ. Proverbs 27:6 affirms *"faithful are the wounds of a friend."* It is a genuine act of love when one Christian corrects another, desiring God's best in the other's life. Members who belong to a church don't sit idly by letting their brothers and sisters continue in sin. They "speak the truth in love" to help others grow into the fullness of Christ (Ephesians 4:15).

The topic of accountability often leads to the topic of church discipline. Jesus provided a means of correction and confrontation in Matthew 18:15-18:

> *If your brother sins against you, go and show him his fault, just between the two of you. If he listens to you, you have won your brother over. But if he will not listen, take one or two others along, so that 'every matter may be established by the testimony of two or three witnesses.' If he refuses to listen to them, tell it to the church; and if he refuses to listen even to the church, treat him as you would a pagan or a tax collector. I tell you the truth, whatever you bind on earth will be bound in heaven, and whatever you loose on earth will be loosed in heaven.*

Notice the progression described in these verses. If a person has sinned against another, the offended party should bring the issue to light. For the sake of unity (see above), maturing believers seek reconciliation (Matthew 5:23-24). If the offender refuses to listen, the brother or sister should return with another for wisdom and accountability. If the offender obstinately refuses to accept responsibility, church leaders should be brought into the matter and the offender removed from the comfort of Christian community.

There are several reasons why Jesus would be so severe in dealing with sinners. The primary reason is restoration. Confrontation hopes for correction. The purpose of church discipline isn't punishment, but to turn sinners back to the way they should go. James reminds us, *"My brothers, if one of you should wander from the truth and someone should bring him back, remember this: Whoever turns a sinner from the error of his way will save him from death and cover over a multitude of sins"* (James 5:19-20).

Another reason for discipline is love. Repeatedly, the Bible affirms that *"the Lord disciplines those He loves"* (Hebrews 12:6, Proverbs 3:12, Job 5:17, Revelation 3:19). If God did not care for us, He would let each of us go our own way. Just as parents dare to correct their children to ensure their success later, so our heavenly Father is determined to discipline His children in love. And, as God's people, we prove our love for each other, not by ignoring sin, but by holding each other accountable and enacting discipline when necessary.

Church discipline also sets a high standard of holiness for the rest of the Body. When sin is unaddressed in the church—gossip, sexual impurity, contention, lying, unfaithfulness or false teaching, for example—it begins to corrode the church. It fractures relationships, limits ministry momentum and presents a poor witness of the church to the world. Most importantly, it distorts the goal of righteous living. Eventually, morality becomes relative, with everyone doing what's right in their own eyes, and leadership loses any standard of holding anyone accountable. Church discipline reminds church members of our high standard of holiness in all things at all times.

The process of church discipline is described in several biblical texts. Jesus teaches that confrontation must be done personally and under the authority of church leadership (Matthew 18:15-20). Paul explains that it should be done gently (Galatians 6:1). The sinning Christian who refuses to repent must be exposed before the church membership (1 Timothy 5:19-20) and refused the joy of fellowship (Matthew 18:17, 1 Corinthians 5:11, 2 Thessalonians 3:14, Titus 3:10). The goal in refusing fellowship is that the one under discipline will miss the benefits of living in biblical community, turn from their sin and return to life with God (see James 5:20).

## A Word About Reconciliation

In his excellent book *The Hole in Our Gospel*, Richard Stearns tells a heartwarming story of Margaret Achiro. Six months pregnant, Margaret was working in her garden when a group of child soldiers, recruited into the Lord's Resistance Army of northern Uganda, emerged from the bush to steal food and supplies. The soldiers began to hack several other women with machetes, but the commander spared Margaret's life because he considered it bad luck to kill a pregnant woman. Instead, he gave orders for the boys to cut off Margaret's ears, nose and lips.

Miraculously, Margaret was rushed to a hospital, saved and gave birth to a baby boy. Months later, the LRS commander who had ordered her attack was captured and brought to the same rehabilitation center. Margaret recognized him and felt the anxiety, fear and anger from the past welling up.

Stearns writes, *"What happened next can only be understood through the miracle of God's love—as a demonstration of the incredible power of the Gospel to redeem even the darkest kinds of evil."* Counselors worked tirelessly with the commander, helping him to admit his atrocities. At the same time, counselors helped Margaret until, finally, a meeting between attacker and victim was arranged. When the two met, Margaret supernaturally found the will to forgive. On the wall of that center is a picture of him, holding baby James.

Indeed, the Gospel has the power to "redeem the darkest kinds of evil." At the cross of Jesus is not only *our* forgiveness, but the capacity for us to forgive others who have hurt us deeply. And, because the church of Jesus is made up of rebels who have each committed the darkest kinds of evil against God but have been reconciled to Him (Romans 5:1, Colossians 1:21-22), we each have the power to be reconciled to one another.

And reconciliation is essential for the church.

One of the most painful experiences of my life was a conflict I endured with another Christian while serving in ministry. Tensions began to arise between me and her regarding how decisions should be made for our organization. In one difficult conversation, she said to me, "Some others in our group don't trust you."

I was shocked and immediately suggested that I should relinquish my leadership role if I was, indeed, considered untrustworthy. Because we were unable to come to a good resolution, I did step down. However, I learned at the next team meeting that she didn't fairly represent to the others why I stepped down. In the end, others misunderstood and thought I lacked commitment to our ministry.

Christian leaders might not be surprised at misrepresentation in the world, but not from their brothers and sisters in the church. I was mad, disappointed and painfully hurt. Ironically, the mentoring ministry we served frequently coached people to "be reconciled" to one another! But, even we had difficulty being restored to one another.

Like most people who feel that they have been offended, I carried bitterness for a while. I wanted justice, not reconciliation. But the Gospel redeems even the darkest kinds of evil. So, I reached out to restore what had been broken. How I hoped my sister in Christ would be eager to reconcile. But, much hurt was still present and the conflict was left unresolved.

While I wish that we could always come to a peaceable reunion, reconciliation isn't always possible. Still, Christians should seek to live at peace with everyone, so far as it depends on them (Romans 12:18). Rather than turn away from conflict, we should march right into it and make amends. Otherwise, the beautiful tapestry of the church suffers an unsightly hole.

Reconciliation begins at the cross of Jesus. As I stand before my Savior who died for me, the cross reminds me of two things: who I was and who I am. First, the cross remind me of who I was. Paul writes, *"Once you were alienated from God and were enemies in your minds because of your evil behavior"* (Colossians 1:21). Isaiah declares, *"We all, like sheep, have gone astray, each of us has turned to his own way; and the Lord has laid on him the iniquity of us all"* (Isaiah 53:6). For me to forgive any sin against me I must remember that I was a sinner first. I stand in the shadow of the cross and look up and see the violence of thorns and nails, the heaving chest of the Son of Man trying to get a breath, the injustice of Jesus' execution, the inconsolable sobs of His mother, and the darkness that enveloped Calvary, and I am reminded that this is because of me. I remember who I was.

But I also remember who I am. *"Therefore, if anyone is in Christ, he is a new creation; the old has gone, the new has come!"* (2 Corinthians 5:17). The cross of Jesus has made me brand new, a renovated person. This means that I have been given a new position (right with God, Romans 5:1), a new purpose (minister of reconciliation, 2 Corinthians 5:18), and a new power (ability to live the life of Jesus, Galatians 2:20). So, the cross of Jesus not only makes it possible for the Christian to forgive, it makes it plausible. It's because of who I am.

The church of Jesus Christ would be a much better place if all its members were patient with one another, forgiving whatever grievances they have against one another, just as the Lord forgave them (Colossians 3:13). To belong to the church means that a person perseveres in and preserves community. For this reason, reconciliation is essential.

## SUMMARY

This chapter helps the Christian to take the next step in the spiritual pathway: Belonging to church. Because the church is a mixed group, a process of membership is important to help leadership know who professes to be a true believer and those who are simply attendees. Membership is also the way Christians express their commitment to the mission of their church. Membership commitments include unity, community, ministry, generosity, authority and accountability. When members neglect their responsibility and stray from the path, other members and leaders enact discipline to restore them and eagerly pursue reconciliation.

## TAKE THE NEXT STEP

1. Are you a member of your church? Why or why not? Has this chapter persuaded you of the value in belonging to your church? If so, take the next step by learning about membership in your church.

2. Do you think the membership expectations of unity, community, ministry, generosity, authority and accountability are too strict? Why or why not? How would you change this list?

3. Why do you think so few churches enact church discipline? What happens to a church that neglects discipline? Do you think that the biblical mandate to be reconciled contradicts the necessity of discipline?

4. What is the most important thing you learned from this chapter?

# BECOME: TRANSFORMATION (PART 1)

*The Creator is a Renovator. He turns trash into treasure and*
*resurrects gems out of rusted junk heaps.*
Unknown

I travelled to Cuba with my missionary friend, Manny Fernandez, and was instantly struck by the beauty of the countryside, the genuine hospitality of the people, the flavor of the local food and the nostalgia of so many classic automobiles. Havana looked like it was frozen in time, its streets filled with vintage American cars built before Castro's revolution and the United States' embargo of 1960. Over the last 55 years, Cuban mechanics have had little access to new parts and have been forced to improvise to keep their "yank tanks" drivable.

Still, the results are extraordinary. Old Buicks, Fords, Chevrolets and Pontiacs have been returned to their former glory. New paint, refurbished interiors and polished chrome details reflect the skill of true artisans. The old has been made new. Each car is a remarkable restoration.

Our God is a renovator. He has a plan to take the junk heap of humanity and restore each person to the former, original glory in-

| BELONG | | | BECOME | | BEYOND | | |
|---|---|---|---|---|---|---|---|
| TO CHRIST | TO COMMUNITY | TO CHURCH | INCIDENTAL TRANSFORMATION | INTENTIONAL TRANSFORMATION | INTO MY CHURCH | INTO MY NEIGHBORHOOD | INTO MY WORLD |

tended for humanity. This work of life transformation is the next step on the spiritual pathway. It is the place where people BECOME who God created them to be.

The first step, BELONG, is the laboratory for the second step, BECOME. When people belong to Christ, the Holy Spirit of God begins to change them from the inside out. As they belong to community, they have opportunity to be challenged by others who are also on their spiritual journeys. Life change happens as they practice the 7 Functions of Biblical Community. Finally, belonging to a church puts them under the authority of spiritual leadership and in a place where they can grow in godliness. In summary, people will not likely BECOME who God intends them to be unless they BELONG.

## You are New

From the day you placed your faith in Jesus, belonged to Him and began your life with God, you were changed. Paul affirms, *"Therefore, if anyone is in Christ, he is a new creation; the old has gone, the new has come!"* (2 Corinthians 5:17). The Christian is renewed. Each one is a new creation, renovated by God. While there are many dimensions of this life change, several are particularly important.

**New vitality.** Spiritually, the Christian has been resurrected from death to life. In Ephesians 2:4-5, Paul announces, *"because of his great love for us, God, who is rich in mercy, made us alive with Christ even when we were dead in transgressions."* Similarly, in Romans 8:10-11, Paul writes,

> But if Christ is in you, your body is dead because of sin, yet your spirit is alive because of righteousness. And if the Spirit of him who raised Jesus from the dead is living in you, he who raised Christ from the dead will also give life to your mortal bodies through his Spirit, who lives in you.

Jesus states in John 5:24, *"I tell you the truth, whoever hears my word and believes him who sent me has eternal life and will not be condemned; he has crossed over from death to life."* Christians have a new vitality, a spiritually new life. This means they are "alive" to the commands of

God and sensitive to the Spirit of God. They possess a living faith (Galatians 2:20) and a living hope (1 Peter 1:3) which produces joy, boldness, endurance, patience and peace.

**New identity.** As mentioned in chapter 2, our identity *before* belonging to Jesus Christ was devastating. We were all sinners (Romans 3:23), separated from God (Ephesians 2:12), enemies of Jesus (Philippians 3:18), lawless rebels (Titus 2:14) and haters of God (Romans 1:30). No matter what our education, our position, our vocation or our nationality, this is who we *were*, separated from God.

But, we were washed, sanctified and justified in the name of the Lord Jesus and by the Spirit of God (1 Corinthians 6:11). In other words, we're not who we were. Our identity has been changed. We are now sons of God (Galatians 3:26), children of God (1 John 3:1), heirs to the kingdom of God (Romans 8:17), friends of God (John 15:15) and free from accusation (Colossians 1:22). This is our new identity.

**New ability.** Once separated from God, people could only live according to the flesh and could only accomplish what their sinful humanity could accomplish. But, in Christ, the Christian has a new power. Indwelled by the Holy Spirit who raised Jesus from the dead, every believer has the supernatural power to walk by faith, surrender to God, and live a victorious life over sin. Jesus said, *"Apart from me, you can do nothing"* (John 15:5) and Paul confidently declared, *"I can everything through Him who gives me strength"* (Philippians 4:13).

**New liberty.** It is popular for people talk about free will as if all human beings have the liberty to do anything they wish. The Bible states otherwise. We are, in fact, dead in our trespasses and sins (Ephesians 2:1), slaves to sin (Romans 6:20) and prisoners in the world (Galatians 3:23). So, while we may do whatever we wish, our sin nature makes it impossible for us to "wish" to do anything righteous and pleasing to God.

Fortunately, *"through Christ Jesus the law of the Spirit of life set me free from the law of sin and death"* (Romans 8:2). Because of the cross, the Christian has a new ability to love what's good, seek what's good and do what's good. No longer in bondage to the old nature and the mastery of sin, the believer has the liberty to live a life pleasing to God.

**New destiny.** Jesus stated that His mission was to "seek and save the lost" (Luke 19:10). Before faith, a person is wandering, without a home, without security, without direction. But the one who belongs to Christ is safe, secure and enjoys a life of purpose. Though the Christian is attacked and accused by the devil, who wishes to cast doubt on their eternal destiny, believers may humbly and confidently defend themselves with,

> *For I am convinced that neither death nor life, neither angels nor demons, neither the present nor the future, nor any powers, neither height nor depth, nor anything else in all creation, will be able to separate us from the love of God that is in Christ Jesus our Lord.* (Romans 8:38-39)

Our new vitality, new identity, new ability, new liberty and new destiny describe what has already been accomplished for us and in us by the death and resurrection of Jesus Christ. John Newton, writer of the great hymn "Amazing Grace," summarizes our past, gracious restoration this way:

> *I am not what I ought to be—ah, how imperfect and deficient! I am not what I wish to be—I abhor what is evil, and I would cleave to what is good! I am not what I hope to be—soon, soon shall I put off mortality, and with mortality all sin and imperfection. Yet, though I am not what I ought to be, nor what I wish to be, nor what I hope to be, I can truly say, I am not what I once was; a slave to sin and Satan; and I can heartily join with the apostle, and acknowledge, "By the grace of God I am what I am!"*

By God's grace, every Christian has been changed. However, our transformation isn't just a past tense event. It is a present tense reality. In 2 Corinthians 3, Paul compares the greater glory of the New Covenant with the limited glory of the Old Covenant. In verse 13, Paul explains, *"We are not like Moses, who would put a veil over his face to keep the Israelites from gazing at it while the radiance was fading away."* Moses experienced a diminishing glory, but God's people today experience a permanent and increasing glory.

After a brief discussion about how the Holy Spirit unveils the truth to God's people, Paul writes, *"And we, who with unveiled faces all reflect the Lord's glory, are being transformed into his likeness with ever-increasing glory, which comes from the Lord, who is the Spirit"* (v. 18). This verse is very informative regarding a theology of change. It highlights four important truths about transformation.

## TRUTH #1
*Transformation is an Ongoing Process*

Nothing matures instantly. Trees begin life as seeds. Butterflies experience metamorphosis from egg to caterpillar to pupa to adult butterfly. Even buildings must begin with a foundation, then walls, then flooring, electrical and plumbing and, eventually, paint and furniture. This principle is true of the spiritual life as well. We are "being transformed" and with "ever-increasing glory" (literally, "from one degree of glory to another"). Our life change takes time…actually, a *lifetime.*

The Bible calls this ongoing change the Christian's sanctification. The word, from the Latin *sanctus*, means "to make holy." It's the life-long process of becoming righteous. We get a better understanding of sanctification when we put it in context of justification and glorification.

Justification is the moment of salvation. It is the work of God in a person that happens in an instant. When an individual hears the Gospel truth and expresses personal faith in Jesus Christ, God declares them *positionally* righteous. That is, they are pronounced "not guilty" in regard to their legal and moral status. Now a Christian, a person is named a son of God, an heir to His promises and eternally secure. They are justified by grace, through faith.

Glorification is the moment of complete salvation when a person dies. In the presence of God there is no condemnation. Rather, each Christian is finally transformed as a new creation. At the second coming of Jesus, their resurrected body is united with their eternal soul and they live in the presence of God, forever renewed. This glorious work is accomplished completely by God.

Between the first moment of justification and the final moment of our glorification is "all of life." This span of time is what we know as the Christian's sanctification. Having been *declared* holy, they now grow experientially in holiness day by day. This process is the cooperative work of the person and the Holy Spirit alive in them. One man said that sanctification is learning to *be* who we already *are*.

Because Christians still live in a corrupt world and because the sin nature in us has been debilitated, but not annihilated, temptation and sin continue to be a challenge. Even the maturing believer will experience seasons of spiritual success and failure. The "graph of spiritual growth" is never a continuous line upward, but a zigzag line filled with peaks and valleys that represent the Christian's success and struggle with sin.

Before the introduction of digital photography, film had to be "developed" in a darkroom in order for an image to be seen. The photographic image was recorded on film the moment the shutter snapped. But, only under exposure to developing chemicals would the final image gradually appear. Photographic labs refer to this as "processing." In the same way, God has determined that He will restore His image in us. We are God's children, but *"what we will be has not yet been made known"* (1 John 3:2). We are continually being developed. Our sanctification is an ongoing process.


# TRUTH #2
### *Transformation is Produced by the Spirit*

In Hollywood, the producer oversees the budget, film scheduling, cast selection, production and marketing of a movie. In short, the producer is the primary supervisor of the movie's success. In the ongoing drama of our life transformation, we have a capable Producer: the Holy Spirit. Because Paul writes that we are *being transformed*, we must realize that transformation is happening *to* us; we do not change ourselves. Rather, the agent of our transformation is "the Lord, who is the Spirit."

There are two opposite but coordinate truths regarding the Holy

Spirit and life change. First, if you don't have the Spirit of God, you cannot be changed. A person can attend self-help groups, counseling sessions, read books, make resolutions or take medication. But total life change is only possible through the power of the Holy Spirit of God.

The prophet Ezekiel received a fantastic vision regarding Israel's restoration after captivity in Babylon. He was transported "by the Spirit of the Lord" into a valley of dry bones (Ezekiel 37:1-2). In ancient times, armies stationed themselves in the hills and would descend into the valley to fight. Dry bones scattered across the valley floor were evidence of defeat and a long period of lifelessness. The Lord asked the prophet, "Son of man, can these bones live?" (v. 3). Humanly speaking, could he imagine the restoration of those who had been defeated?

Ezekiel answered, *"O Sovereign LORD, you alone know."* Only according to His sovereign will and power could God raise the dead.

Then, the Lord commanded Ezekiel,

*"Prophesy to these bones and say to them, 'Dry bones, hear the word of the LORD! This is what the Sovereign LORD says to these bones: I will make breath enter you, and you will come to life. I will attach tendons to you and make flesh come upon you and cover you with skin; I will put breath in you, and you will come to life. Then you will know that I am the LORD.' "* (Ezekiel 37:4-6)

So, the prophet obeyed and preached to the pile of lifeless bones, and soon something began to happen. Bones began to rattle. Muscle, tendon and flesh covered them and the reconstituted beings took the form of life, but *"there was no breath in them"* (v. 8). A human being without breath may look alive, but lack the fundamental animating power for life. A person without breath is said to be dead.

Next, the Lord commanded Ezekiel, *"Prophesy to the breath; prophesy, son of man, and say to it, 'This is what the Sovereign LORD says: Come from the four winds, O breath, and breathe into these slain, that they may live.'"* (v. 9). So he preached and the lifeless beings stood up, a vast army of the Lord.

Ezekiel's vision was intended to teach an important spiritual truth. Preaching, by itself, does not change a person. Proclamation doesn't end in resurrection. What lifeless people need is "breath." It's important to understand that the Hebrew word for "breath" may also be translated "wind" or "spirit." Breath is needed for natural life. But the Spirit is necessary for supernatural life. For this reason, the Lord said, *"I will put my Spirit in you and you will live, and I will settle you in your own land. Then you will know that I the LORD have spoken, and I have done it, declares the LORD"* (v. 14).

A pastor, preaching on Ezekiel 37, said "At the end of every human effort, there is still death." Jesus said, *"The Spirit gives life; the flesh counts for nothing"* (John 6:63). This means change only comes by the Holy Spirit. And, a person who doesn't have the Spirit cannot be changed.

The opposite principle is also true: If you have the Spirit of God, you *will* be changed. Just as a movie producer is intent on making a movie a success, so the Holy Spirit is intent on producing successful life transformation in the believer. The apostle Paul assures us, *"And if the Spirit of him who raised Jesus from the dead is living in you, he who raised Christ from the dead will also give life to your mortal bodies through his Spirit, who lives in you"* (Romans 8:11).

There are various proofs of the Holy Spirit's work in a person:

**The Holy Spirit produces character.** The fruit, or evidence, of the Holy Spirit's work is *"love, joy, peace, patience, kindness, goodness, faithfulness, gentleness and self-control"* (Galatians 5:22-23). A person who is being changed by the Spirit will increasingly show this fruit.

**The Holy Spirit produces conviction.** Jesus said, *"When [the Spirit] comes, he will convict the world of guilt in regard to sin and righteousness and judgment"* (John 16:8). A person sensitive to the Holy Spirit will be conscious of sin, have genuine sorrow over sin and exercise repentance from sin.

**The Holy Spirit produces confidence.** *"May the God of hope fill you with all joy and peace as you trust in him, so that you may overflow with hope by the power of the Holy Spirit"* (Romans 15:13). People filled and changed by the Holy Spirit possess a hope for their eternal future that strengthens their hearts and gives them confidence for the future.

**The Holy Spirit produces contentment.** Paul writes, *"...the mind controlled by the Spirit is life and peace"* (Romans 8:6). Because we have peace with God through Jesus (Romans 5:1), Christians are free from anxiety and rest with confidence in their standing before Him.

**The Holy Spirit produces comprehension.** *"But when he, the Spirit of truth, comes, he will guide you into all truth"* (John 16:13). Jesus promised the "Helper" who would remind His people of what He taught and enable them to understand. On the other hand, the person without the Holy Spirit cannot understand spiritual truths (1 Corinthians 2:12-14).

**The Holy Spirit produces compassion.** *"If you have any encouragement from being united with Christ, if any comfort from his love, if any fellowship with the Spirit, if any tenderness and compassion..."* (Philippians 2:1). Our union with the Holy Spirit produces a compassion for others and a desire to meet their needs, not only our own.

Clearly, the Holy Spirit is central to the work of life transformation. A pastor once shared an illustration with his congregation about this truth. He said, "You can make a balloon rise in the air by hitting it with your hand or filling it with helium. Some leaders think they should 'smack' their people to get them to do what's right. But, if their people are filled with the Holy Spirit, they will rise to higher levels of maturity. Sanctification is the whole work of God from the inside out."

# TRUTH #3

*Our Transformation Pattern is Jesus Christ*

Before moving into vocational ministry, I studied to be a graphic designer. In basic art classes, especially in painting, the artist is taught to "paint what he sees." That is, the artist sets up an arrangement of fruit (for example), and pays close attention to his subject in order to translate the image on canvas. Keeping his eyes on the original, the artist learns to reproduce a reasonable copy.

When God changes a life, He has a particular picture in mind: the image of His Son, Jesus Christ. In 2 Corinthians 3:18, Paul states that the Christian is being changed "into His likeness." In Romans 8:29, he also writes, *"those God foreknew he also predestined to be conformed to the likeness of His Son."* And, in Colossians 3:9-10, he states, *"...you have taken off your old self with its practices and have put on the new self, which is being renewed in knowledge in the image of its Creator."*

Because Jesus was perfectly human, He is the prototype of all people. The "first Adam" was corrupted by sin, and so everyone born after him shares his sinful image. Jesus is the "last Adam" (1 Corinthians 15:45), the Father's sinless, spotless Son, and is the model of what God intends for all human beings. Little by little, the Spirit of God gives us the mind of Christ, the heart of Christ and the life of Christ so that we look less like our old self and become more like our Savior.

In the classic story of "Beauty and the Beast," a young prince refuses kindness to an old beggar woman at his door and is cursed with a miserable, beastly condition until he discovers love. As time is running out for the curse to be removed, he meets a beautiful girl from the local village who begins to show the beast unconditional love and acceptance despite who he appears to be. Through the girl's enduring love, the beast is finally transformed to the handsome prince he was born to be.

The Christian is born under the curse of sin and destined for a miserable, beastly life apart from God. Through His loving sacrifice, Jesus breaks the curse by taking the curse on Himself. The Holy Spirit restores us to our original condition, transforming us into the person we were born to be—not like the first Adam, but like the last Adam, the pattern of Jesus Christ.

This transformation will not be complete until we stand in Jesus' presence. The Apostle John looked forward with hope:

> *Dear friends, now we are children of God, and what we will be has not yet been made known. But we know that when he appears, we shall be like him, for we shall see him as he is. Everyone who has this hope in him purifies himself, just as he is pure.* (1 John 3:2-3)

Likewise, Paul imagines the total transformation of our bodies:

> *But our citizenship is in heaven. And we eagerly await a Savior from*

*there, the Lord Jesus Christ, who, by the power that enables him to bring everything under his control, will transform our lowly bodies so that they will be like his glorious body.* (Philippians 3:20-21)

## TRUTH #4
*Our Transformation Purpose is the Glory of God*

In order to understand this final principle, we must remember God's *original* design of humanity. After creating the world, God chose to create man "in His image" (Genesis 1:26). That is, people were created by God to reflect the glory of God. God didn't need people. He wasn't lonely. Rather, He chose to create us so that people would communicate—relationally, emotionally, intellectually, volitionally, metaphysically and ethically—something of what God is like. We were created for *His* glory (Isaiah 43:7).

In the same way, we were *recreated* for God's glory.

When Adam sinned, the glory of God in man was contaminated. No longer did people perfectly point back to the beauty, power, love, freedom, unity and holiness of their Creator. Sin obscured our reflection of the glory of God. But, in Jesus Christ, *"the old has gone, the new has come"* (2 Corinthians 5:17). The Christian has been called out of darkness and into the light of God in order to *"declare His praises"* (1 Peter 2:9). Those God foreknew *"he also predestined to be conformed to the likeness of his Son"* so that Jesus might be gloriously exalted in supremacy (Romans 8:29). We were chosen before the foundation of the world and adopted as God's sons *"for the praise of His glorious grace"* (Ephesians 1:4-6). As recreated people, our lives can glorify God once again.

This means that our transformation becomes our exaltation. The more that we are changed, the more we worship God. Every part of us that gets renewed points back to our Renewer and honors Him, not us.

My son Pearson invited me to attend a professional ice hockey game featuring a team that he liked. I wore jeans and a t-shirt, but he wore a hockey jersey with the insignia of the team. When we arrived at the arena, I was clearly in the minority. Virtually every fan wore green and white—shirts, ball caps, jackets and souvenir foam fingers. Clothed in the team colors, they proved that they supported the team and, when I looked around the arena, the great sea of green and white made the *team* look greater, not the fans.

The Bible states that Christians have "clothed themselves with the Lord Jesus Christ" (Galatians 3:27, Romans 13:14). We have donned the colors of our Savior. And, as our life is changed to look like Him, our appearance doesn't honor us, but Him. Pastor John Piper writes, "As we are conformed to the image of Christ, He is made more and more the center of all things." Christ in us makes Christ look good.

## Changed on Purpose

Because God is intent on changing our lives, this too is the mission of the church. The church is not in the business of *religion*, but *reformation*. As we think about the spiritual pathway, this second step where the Christian BECOMES more like Jesus has two important aspects the Christian should understand: incidental vs. intentional life transformation.

### *Incidental Transformation*

Many Christians are content with *incidental* life transformation. This is change that happens "along the way." It's not purposeful, but accidental, so to speak. It's like reading a book at a coffee café for several hours. When you leave, you discover that your clothing retains the aroma of coffee. You didn't *try* to smell like coffee; it's just the by-product of having sat in the vicinity of coffee for a time.

The formula of Time + Frequency + Influence = Change holds true most of the time in the church. The more time people spend in the church, the greater likelihood they have of experiencing change. The more frequently they participate in spiritual exercises, the greater likelihood they have of experiencing change. And, the more influential encounters they have (powerful sermons, spiritual friends, helpful counseling), the greater likelihood they have of experiencing change. Jesus' disciples were changed because they were with Him for three years, sat daily under His teaching and experienced the influence of His character, truth and miracles. Later, the religious officials observed that Peter and John were "unschooled, ordinary fishermen" but noted that they had "been with Jesus" (Acts 4:13). Just being with Jesus brought change.

As we participate in the life and ministry of our church, we should expect that we will experience incidental life change. We may never know exactly *how* we are changed or *how much* we are changed, but we should expect that it is better to belong to community and church because these are the environments of change.

The reality of incidental transformation should also remind us of the influence our lives have, even when we're not trying. Parents know that their children are the products of their environments, learning how to be generous, compassionate, prideful or materialistic without ever having been specifically "taught." People "absorb" the culture where they live. So, as we do life with others, we must beware that our lives are always leading, discipling others in one direction or the other.

The problem with incidental life transformation is that it doesn't often produce the substantive life change that God desires for our lives. A person who attends church most Sundays, gives an offering and attends a Bible study will likely grow more than a person who doesn't do any of those things. But the change they experience is more like preventative maintenance that simply ensures a house is maintained in livable, safe conditions than total renovation that radically changes every aspect of a home to make it better.

While incidental transformation is inevitable and desirable, it's not the greatest transformation that God intends for our lives.

## *Intentional Transformation*

Though many Christians are content with incidental or "accidental" life change, God wants us to actively seek it. His will is that we be sanctified (1 Thessalonians 4:3) and that we choose to no longer be conformed to the patterns of this world but be transformed by the renewing of our minds (Romans 12:1-2). This is not something that happens accidently or passively, but is the result of intentional, deliberate, persistent pursuit of holiness by God's people. This is the topic that we will cover in greater detail in the next chapter.

## SUMMARY

The Renaissance sculptor Michelangelo Buonarroti was asked why he was working so hard to move a slab of stone. He replied, "I saw an angel in the marble and carved until I set him free." This chapter has explored the commitment of God to bring about the Christian's total life change. From the moment we first encountered God, He changed our vitality, identity, ability, liberty and destiny. But, God intends our *past* transformation to have effect in the *present*. Sanctification is a process "with ever-increasing glory." It is a work of the Holy Spirit producing spiritual maturity in the believer. God's goal for us is to conform us to the pattern or image of His Son, Jesus. And, His ultimate goal is His own glory—magnifying Himself through the restoration of His people.

## TAKE THE NEXT STEP

1. Review the list of how God has already changed you—a new vitality, identity, ability, liberty and destiny. Which of these do you easily embrace and affirm? Which one is more difficult to understand? Why?

2. In what way has God changed your life since the moment you first believed in Jesus? What factors were part of the "process" by which that change happened?

3. Several "proofs" of the Holy Spirit's sanctifying work were given (pages 84-85). Evaluate each of these for your own life. Which of these are apparent in your own life and which are not? Why?

4. Too often, Christians are encouraged to be changed, but Jesus is not the pattern or goal. What other illegitimate "images" are held up as patterns for Christians?

5. Why do you think God wishes to change your life?

6. What is the most important thing you learned from this chapter?

# BECOME: TRANSFORMATION (PART 2)

*Do not conform any longer to the pattern of this world,*
*but be transformed by the renewing of your mind...*
Romans 12:2

I recently crossed the mid-century mark of 50 years old. Looking back over my life, I can't remember a time when I "got older" or "grew up." What I mean is that I can recall being 10 years old and playing cops and robbers with my best friend in Georgia. I can also remember my family moving to Texas when I was 11 years old. I remember the experience of sitting in my first seminary class at age 25 and receiving my diploma almost three years later when I was 27. But, I have no recollection of the transition from 10 to 11 or the time between 25 and 27. I was becoming mature but didn't realize it.

We could say I have grown *incidentally* over the last 50 years. I haven't been entirely conscious of my progress. I didn't try to get taller, for example, nor did I realize it was happening at a particular time. But, looking back, I can see the progress.

In the last chapter, we looked at the common experience of incidental life transformation that many Christians enjoy. But, God's goal for us is not to simply look back and notice our growth, but to active-

| BELONG | | | BECOME | | BEYOND | | |
|---|---|---|---|---|---|---|---|
| TO CHRIST | TO COMMUNITY | TO CHURCH | INCIDENTAL TRANSFORMATION | INTENTIONAL TRANSFORMATION | INTO MY CHURCH | INTO MY NEIGHBORHOOD | INTO MY WORLD |

ly participate in it. We must be *intentional* to walk further along the spiritual pathway to maturity.

Jesus said to His disciples, *"If anyone would come after me, he must deny himself and take up his cross and follow me"* (Matthew 16:24). A "disciple" is a learner, a pupil or an apprentice. It's someone who "comes after" a master. No one accidently or expectantly becomes a disciple of Jesus any more than someone accidently becomes a farmer or a doctor or a police officer. We consciously choose to follow Jesus which means a daily and deliberate decision to "deny ourselves" and "take up our cross" and "follow Him."

This is what Paul emphasizes to the Philippian Christians. The Apostle had visited the church on his second missionary journey. While he was there, he preached the Gospel, baptized new converts, trained leaders and established a church. Paul stayed a while and guided the young believers in their newfound faith and instructed them in what to believe and how to live. Eventually, however, Paul moved on to new missionary frontiers and left the church to take responsibility for its own maturity.

This reminds me of my own spiritual journey while in college. Having trusted in Jesus a month before my high school graduation, I entered college as a newborn Christian. Quickly I discovered friends, campus clubs, a church and Bible studies that helped me grow exponentially during the next four years. I joined a group of 20 other college men and we established a new Christian fraternity based on brotherhood and unity. The field of my heart was fertile, and multiple layers of worship, prayer groups, theological conversations, conferences, mission trips and leadership opportunities established a solid foundation for the rest of my life.

Then I graduated.

I stayed in the city where I attended college, but many of my friends moved away. I was no longer in our great fraternity. My day was no longer saturated with spiritual conversations. I worked five days a week and had bills to pay. It was a whole new world where I was going to have to take personal responsibility for my spiritual growth.

During this time, I memorized 1 Peter 3:15, *"Always be prepared to give an answer to everyone who asks you to give the reason for the hope that you have."* This simple verse reminded me that I needed to live my hope and defend my hope, but before either could happen, I had to *own* my hope. It had to become *the hope I have*, not the hope of my parents, my church, my friends or the clubs I enjoyed. In short, I had to take ownership of my faith.

So, as Paul left the Philippians, they faced an opportunity. Like babies who must eventually leave their mother's breast and begin eating for themselves, it was time for them to no longer live off the faith of Paul, but to own their faith. With this, Paul wrote,

> *Therefore, my dear friends, as you have always obeyed—not only in my presence, but now much more in my absence—continue to work out your salvation with fear and trembling, for it is God who works in you to will and to act according to his good purpose.* (Philippians 2:12-13)

This verse highlights three important principles to remember regarding intentional life transformation in the Christian.


1

*We Work Out Our Salvation. We Don't Work for It.*

This is one of many examples where word meanings matter when reading the Bible. Two countries work *for* a treaty and then, after the treaty has been signed, they work *out* their individual responsibilities. Similarly, a couple works *for* (or toward) their marriage and then they spend the rest of their lives working *out* how to live with and love one another day by day.

This verse in no way suggests that a person may gain salvation by works. Clearly, the Bible dismisses any human effort in regard to our favor with God. Paul writes, *"For it is by grace you have been saved, through faith—and this not from yourselves, it is the gift of God—not by works, so that no one can boast"* (Ephesians 2:8-9). In 2 Timothy 1:9, Paul likewise writes that God *"saved us and called us to a holy life—not because of anything we have done but because of his own purpose and grace."* Salvation is never by human work.

But, once saved, Christians *do* "work out" the particulars of life with God. The phrase "work out" means "to produce." A non-biblical first century writer used this Greek word in regard to digging for silver. With this in mind, Paul is urging Christians to "mine their salvation." Search for all the treasure to be gained in your life with Jesus.

## 2
### *Our Working Out Begins With God Working In Us.*

Paul commands us to "work out our salvation with fear and trembling" and then adds *"for* it is God who works in you...." We work because God works first. In the last chapter, we discussed the Holy Spirit as the producer of life change. Having believed, the Holy Spirit lives in the Christian and desires to sanctify the Christian through and through. Looking toward the New Covenant, the Lord promised His people,

> *For I will take you out of the nations; I will gather you from all the countries and bring you back into your own land. I will sprinkle clean water on you, and you will be clean; I will cleanse you from all your impurities and from all your idols. I will give you a new heart and put a new spirit in you; I will remove from you your heart of stone and give you a heart of flesh. And I will put my Spirit in you and move you to follow my decrees and be careful to keep my laws.* (Ezekiel 36:24-27)

When God gives people a new heart of flesh, He also gives them His Spirit who compels us to follow God's commands. The result is that no one can take credit for their own spiritual maturity. Every step of growth is because God is at work in the believer and therefore deserves the glory for what He is doing.

## 3
### *Life Change Requires Our Response and Responsibility.*

This gets to the command in this passage. In Paul's absence, Christians needed to take personal responsibility for their spiritual progress. The question is not whether God will do His part, helping Christians understand truth, showing them the path of righteousness, giving them the power to do what God requires, making them sensitive to sin in their lives, leading them to repentance, and enabling them to glorify God in all they do (1 Corinthians 10:31). The question is whether each Christian will take personal responsibility to join God in His work.

During seminary, I took a pastoral counseling course to learn how to help people find freedom from their problems. While the course explored the deeper dimensions of psychology and human behavior, our professor offered a very simple tool for determining whether a person could be helped through counseling. He suggested three questions:

1. Do you know what the problem is?
2. Do you wish to change?
3. Are you willing to do whatever is necessary to change?

These are three very telling questions. No doubt, people face problems every day in which they don't understand what the real problem is (Question #1). I once counseled a man who was overcome with loneliness but didn't realize that he interacted with people in a way that was awkward and made them feel uncomfortable. Another person wanted help with outbursts of anger, but didn't understand that the root was an unhealthy need to be in control. Most people are glad to learn what their "problem" is.

The first question addresses information. But the second question deals with aspiration: What do you want? Some people know what they need to do, but don't really want to do it. Not long ago, I asked a man who struggled with alcohol if he understood that his drinking was damaging his relationships, his job security and his health. He did. But when asked if he wished to change, he much preferred his drinking. Some Christians still prefer their sin habits instead of a life of holiness. And, they will never be free from sin until their desire is changed.

Question #3 is most important. Having learned of their problems and wishing to change, people must be willing to take part in their own progress. While sanctification is the work of God's Spirit, it requires human response and responsibility. In 1 Corinthians 15:10, Paul states *"[B]y the grace of God I am what I am, and his grace to me was not without effect. No, I worked harder than all of them—yet not I, but the grace of God that was with me."* God's grace, freely given to Paul, was "not without effect." That is, God's grace was "at work" helping Paul to work harder.

There are more than a few verses in the Bible that highlight the responsibility of Christians to cooperate in their intentional transformation:

*Do not conform any longer to the pattern of this world, but be transformed by the renewing of your mind.* (Romans 12:2)

*When I was a child, I talked like a child, I thought like a child, I reasoned like a child. When I became a man, I put childish ways behind me.* (1 Corinthians 13:11)

*So I say, live by the Spirit, and you will not gratify the desires of the sinful nature.* (Galatians 5:16)

*You were taught, with regard to your former way of life, to put off your old self, which is being corrupted by its deceitful desires; to be made new in the attitude of your minds; and to put on the new self, created to be like God in true righteousness and holiness.* (Ephesians 4:22-24)

*And we pray this in order that you may live a life worthy of the Lord and may please him in every way: bearing fruit in every good work, growing in the knowledge of God, being strengthened with all power according to his glorious might so that you may have great endurance and patience, and joyfully giving thanks to the Father, who has qualified you to share in the inheritance of the saints in the kingdom of light.* (Colossians 1:10-13)

*So then, just as you received Christ Jesus as Lord, continue to live in him, rooted and built up in him, strengthened in the faith as you were taught, and overflowing with thankfulness. See to it that no one takes you captive through hollow and deceptive philosophy, which depends on human tradition and the basic principles of this world rather than on Christ.* (Colossians 2:6-8)

*Have nothing to do with godless myths and old wives' tales; rather, train yourself to be godly. For physical training is of some value, but godliness has value for all things, holding promise for both the present life and the life to come.* (1 Timothy 4:7-8)

*In fact, though by this time you ought to be teachers, you need someone to teach you the elementary truths of God's word all over again. You need milk, not solid food! Anyone who lives on milk, being still an infant, is not acquainted with the teaching about righteousness. But solid food is for the mature, who by constant use have trained themselves to distinguish good from evil.* (Hebrews 5:12-14)

*Therefore, since we are surrounded by such a great cloud of witnesses, let us throw off everything that hinders and the sin that so easily entangles, and let us run with perseverance the race marked out for us. Let us fix our eyes on Jesus, the author and perfecter of our faith, who for the joy set before him endured the cross, scorning its shame, and sat down at the right hand of the throne of God. Consider him who endured such opposition from sinful men, so that you will not grow weary and lose heart.* (Hebrews 12:1-3)

*As obedient children, do not conform to the evil desires you had when you lived in ignorance. But just as he who called you is holy, so be holy in all you do; for it is written: "Be holy, because I am holy."* (1 Peter 1:14-16)

*[M]ake every effort to add to your faith goodness; and to goodness, knowledge; and to knowledge, self-control; and to self-control, perseverance; and to perseverance, godliness; and to godliness, brotherly kindness; and to brotherly kindness, love... be all the more eager to make your calling and election sure.* (2 Peter 1:5-7)

*Therefore, dear friends, since you already know this, be on your guard so that you may not be carried away by the error of lawless men and fall from your secure position. But grow in the grace and knowledge of our Lord and Savior Jesus Christ.* (2 Peter 3:17-18)

Every command is a challenge. God's people cannot simply expect themselves to be changed because they attend church. God's goal has never been for us to become converts, but disciples—apprentices of Jesus who pursue growth in our life with Him.

## What Must Change

Before moving to specific areas of spiritual growth in the next chapter, it is helpful to look at several dimensions of each person's life and how change may take place. In 1955, American psychologists Joseph Luft and Harrington Ingham developed a diagram to describe how people relate to themselves and others. While this model has been used often in therapeutic or corporate leadership settings, it is very valuable for church leaders wishing to help their people grow and for the disciple who wishes to better understand who they are. The "Johari Window," as it is commonly called, has four "spaces:"

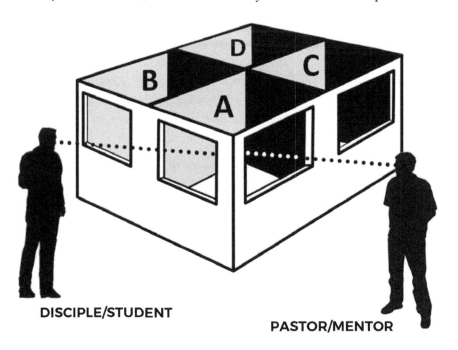

**DISCIPLE/STUDENT**

**PASTOR/MENTOR**

Looking at the big picture of the Johari Window, the observer notices two people who are in relationship with one another. The "building" represents the life of the student. There are some dimensions in the student's life which are visible to both the student and the leader (A). Other dimensions are visible only to the student *or* the teacher (B, C). And one dimension is not immediately visible to either (D). Each of these will be discussed in turn with brief discipleship exercises for the leader.

## PUBLIC IMAGE (A)

A person's "public image" is the picture of themselves they project for others to see. Every person is consciously particular about their public image. In fact, most people are very deliberate to shape, protect and promote a specific image they want others to see.

Sometimes, we refer to a person's public image as a "façade"—a front or outward appearance that is maintained to conceal a less pleasant reality. A businessman may seem generous in his community, but treat his employees unfairly, unkindly and without dignity. A teenager may appear confident and courageous, but may be really masking fear of being out of control. As a result, while our public image is the most frequent image people see, it's not the most accurate.

Therefore, people should not be elevated to ministry leadership based only on an evaluation of their public image. God sent Samuel to anoint the next king over Israel and the prophet was quickly enamored with Jesse's oldest son. But, the Lord warned him, *"Do not consider his appearance or his height, for I have rejected him. The* LORD *does not look at the things man looks at. Man looks at the outward appearance, but the* LORD *looks at the heart"* (1 Samuel 16:7). People always present their "best side" and therefore, no leader should be appointed simply based on their public image. For this reason, Paul cautioned Timothy about being hasty *"in the laying on of hands"* (1 Timothy 5:22).

Recognizing the reality of a person's public image is equally important for discipleship. How people present themselves may not be the true picture of who they are deep within. Judas gave every indication of being trustworthy until he betrayed Jesus. Ananias and his wife, Sapphira, seemed sacrificial and honest when, in fact, they were stingy and were hiding a lie (Acts 5). From the beginning, the devil *"masquerades as an angel of light"* (2 Corinthians 11:14), and those who fall into his temptation seek to cover up their sin (Genesis 3:7-8).

So, as one person disciples or mentors another, they must maintain an appropriate "skepticism" about where people really are on the spiritual pathway. This doesn't mean the leader is judgmental, but that he or she understands that a façade may be covering a more unsightly reality. We help people, not by looking at the surface, but by digging deeper. Like the psalmist, we pray for ourselves and others, *"Search me, O God, and know my heart; test me and know my anxious thoughts. See if there is any offensive way in me, and lead me in the way everlasting"* (Psalm 139:23-24).

**EXERCISE:** *Discover your "public" life by asking 5-7 people who know you well to describe you only using five words. Gather the lists and reflect on the results. Which of these words please you? Which of them surprise you? Why?*

## PRIVATE LIFE (B)

A person's "private life" is the part of their life they see, but others don't perceive. It's private because it's known only to them. And, just as most people are very careful to promote their public image, they are equally careful to protect their private life.

There are several things hidden in the closet of a person's private life. Unspoken hopes and dreams are there. As a college pastor, I met a number of students who were pursuing a career in particular field, not because they wanted to, but because it pleased their parents. Each of us has unspoken dreams, some unfulfilled. For me, I have had a short dream list: Publish a book, skydive at least once, and pray with a sitting President of the United States, to name a few. As interesting or absurd as any dream may be, it's within the heart of a person and drives them.

Also hidden in the private life of a person are their personal fears and insecurities. Few people wish to appear weak, so they bury their fears deeply away from the eyes of others. People are afraid of failure, inadequacy, loneliness, loss of control, not knowing an answer, financial ruin, rejection, debilitating sickness and death, etc. Just as secret dreams drive a person, so secret fears can hold them back.

The most dangerous part of a person's private life is their secret sin. David carried on an affair with Bathsheba, manipulated and murdered her husband and lied about his sin (2 Samuel 11). All of this was unknown to the people who only saw his public leadership. Similarly, God's people today wrestle with habits and hang-ups left over from their old lives. While the reality of sin remains, our attempt to hide it can be devastating. Proverbs 28:13 warns, *"He who conceals his sins does not prosper."* Through His prophet, God cautions,

> *Woe to those who go to great depths*
>> *to hide their plans from the* LORD,
> *who do their work in darkness and think,*
>> *"Who sees us? Who will know?"* (Isaiah 29:15)

So, while a person may successfully conceal their sin from others, they are *"naked and exposed to the eyes of him to whom we must give an account"* (Hebrews 4:13). The disciple must be aware of their tendency to hide their secret hopes, fears and sin, and, for their spiritual progress, bring into the light what has been kept in the dark.

**EXERCISE:** *To explore your "private" life, ask yourself, "What is something I dream about which I have only told few people, if any?" or "What decisions would I make with my life if I were 100% confident of success?" or "What one thing is holding me back from greater spiritual progress?" These questions will help uncover the private life of the disciple.*

## BLIND SPOTS (C)

While driving an automobile, a driver must be very careful of "blind spots." These are obscure areas near the back quarter panels of their car—over the driver's left or right shoulders—where other cars, motorcycles or bicyclists might be riding, out of sight from the driver.

Everyone has blind spots in their personal life. These are areas of growth or development are visible to others, but not to the disciple. Blind spots are behaviors, personality traits, habits, speech patterns or attitudes which are "automatic."

When I first started preaching, my wife would gently give me feedback after each sermon. On one Sunday, she humorously described my delivery as a "machine gun" approach to preaching. At first, I didn't agree with her. I was blind and couldn't see her perspective. It wasn't until other friends shared the same criticism over several months that I had to accept the reality that I talk too fast.

During an annual review several years ago, my Elder Board shared several positive observations about my ministry. But, among the group of advisors, there was a common concern: I needed to delegate ministry instead of taking responsibility for everything. I was blind to this leadership deficiency and began to defend my practices. Eventually, I had to realize that my brothers could see something that I couldn't.

Blind spots aren't always negative. Sometimes, a person has positive qualities that are seen by others, but not by them. The person may be an exceptional servant or have the ability to attract followers. Perhaps they are a volunteer teacher who isn't aware of the quality and impact of their lessons. I once counseled a young man who was being persecuted for his godly passion, and I noted that he demonstrated extraordinary patience and perseverance—qualities not always found in other believers. When leading disciples, it's helpful to affirm how God has made them for ministry and for His glory.

Obviously, identifying positive or negative blind spots is crucial for personal growth. Every disciple needs friends who will gently and honestly point out what they cannot see for themselves. Leaders who help others discover their blind spots demonstrate concern, commitment, and courage, the indispensable virtues of leadership.

**EXERCISE:** *As you grow deeper in your relationship with Jesus, ask yourself, "If there is something about your life which you could not see, but was preventing you from becoming what God wants you to be, would you want to know about it?" This question gives you an opportunity to take inventory of your willingness to mature. Two telling questions may follow: "Who do you trust to tell you the truth about your life, even if it's difficult to hear?" and "If you* *learned something about your life that was preventing your spiritu-al maturity, would you be willing to address it?" If you're willing, ask a trusted, spiritual friend if there are blind spots they see in your life which might be preventing you from growing.*

## UNKNOWN POTENTIAL (D)

This fourth section of the Johari Window is mysterious. It's the part of the disciple's life that is unknown to both the disciple and their leader. This section holds open the possibility that God may call a person to something unexpected or open a door of opportunity un-anticipated. Neither Moses nor his Egyptian father would have guessed that he would become the deliverer to lead God's people out of Egypt. Esther was surprised to learn that she would become a res-cuer of the Jews. Paul never imagined that he would abandon his Jewish legalism and become an apostle to the Gentiles. Peter had no idea, casting his nets into the Sea of Galilee, that he would one day become a fisher of men.

Surely, God knows the plans He has for each person, even if we don't:

*All the days ordained for me were written in your book before one of them came to be.* (Psalm 139:16)

*Before I formed you in the womb I knew you, before you were born I set you apart; I appointed you as a prophet to the nations.* (Jeremiah 1:5)

*For we are God's workmanship, created in Christ Jesus to do good works, which God prepared in advance for us to do.* (Ephesians 2:10)

In every discipleship relationship, the leader must imagine great potential for their apprentice. They must never let present circum-stances or limitations disqualify a disciple from God's possible, fu-ture plans. Just as a 10-year-old cannot imagine that they will one day be closing real estate deals, so the young Christian may not be able to conceive of becoming a missionary, preaching a sermon or evangelizing their community one day. But, with God, all things are possible...and potential.

## Going Public

It is not enough for the disciple to be aware of these four personal dimensions. The goal is for those areas which are obscure to become clear. As the disciple's private life, blind spots and unknown potential are revealed, the disciple begins to live publically more of who they really are. This is an important step in spiritual transformation. This growing public image looks like this:

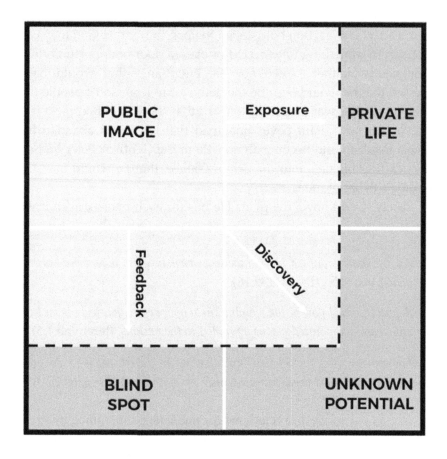

Notice that this growing public reality for the disciple doesn't happen automatically. It is an intentional and cooperative effort between the disciple and a leader, pastor or friend in their community.

The disciple's Private Life diminishes through "exposure." That is, as the student is exposed to God's truth, their sin is exposed before the Body. This isn't for the purpose of shaming any Christian, but so that what is in the dark might be brought into the light. If you are a pastor, this raises an important question for you: Is your church a "safe" place where people may fail? Is your church a place for perfect people or is it a hospital for broken people who are getting healed? Is grace practiced among everyone? If so, believers will be more open to having their private life go public so that they may grow to maturity.

The disciple's Blind Spots are revealed through feedback and coaching. This means that growing Christians must be in community in order to receive these kinds of constructive comments. Trust must be cultivated between relationships in order for a disciple to hear "hard truth" from a friend who reveals their blind spots. This raises more questions for the pastor reading this book: Does your church encourage biblical community where each Christian may be truly "known?" Are you and other leaders courageous in confronting sin within the church? Do you care enough about people to tell them hard truth? Do you as a leader set an example for receiving feedback from others?

The disciple's Unknown Potential is revealed through discovery. Through trial and error and the gentle prodding of a leader, disciples stretch themselves in new experiences. I know several people who dared to travel to a foreign country on a short-term mission trip and learned that they possessed a deep desire to see the Gospel go to the nations. An older man was invited to serve in our children's ministry and discovered that he was effective as a grandfatherly influence. In each case, the individual didn't know they would find success until they ventured into uncharted territory. Once again, several questions are crucial for the pastor: Is your church a place where people are en-couraged to take risks with no fear of reprimand if they fail? Does your church have an means for people to discover their spiritual gifts? Are you willing to allow young, untested or emerging leaders an opportunity to "test" their skills in preaching, teaching, evange-lism, organization and pastoral care? Only in a safe environment with trusted leaders can disciples discover their hidden potential.

## SUMMARY

No Christian should settle for incidental life transformation. Just as Jesus grew in wisdom and stature (Luke 2:52), so each believer must cooperate with the Holy Spirit for their own maturity. Those committed to spiritual growth must be mindful of the multiple dimensions of their life represented by the Johari Window: public image, private life, blind spots and unknown potential. The goal is for the disciple's public image to become more and more of who they truly are, as the other dimensions diminish through personal, intentional growth.

## TAKE THE NEXT STEP

1. In what specific area can you point to the Holy Spirit's work in your life, changing you over time?

2. Name an area of your life where you identified a problem and made an intentional decision to take steps for change. What, specifically, did you do? How did you perceive God at work during this time?

3. If you asked 5 friends to describe you, what words would they use to describe your "public image"? How true is this image to what is inside you, which few ever see?

4. What private dreams do you have? What fears do you have?

5. Without being judgmental, what "blind spots" have you seen in another person? What responsibility did you have to help them see their blind spots and begin moving toward life change?

6. What is the most important thing you learned from this chapter?

# BECOME: TRANSFORMATION (PART 3)

*We can't go on indefinitely being just ordinary, decent eggs.*
*We must be hatched or go bad.*
C.S. Lewis

In the last two chapters, we have considered the importance of life change. God has no intention of allowing His people, purchased by the precious blood of His Son, Jesus, to continue being "ordinary, decent eggs." His goal is to radically change every part of us, by the power of the Holy Spirit, in order for us to become devoted disciples of Jesus.

Having considered *how* God changes a person and each Christian's personal responsibility to cooperate in their life change, we now turn to the ultimate goal. In chapter 5, I wrote that our "transformation pattern is Jesus Christ." But, we need more detail to understand exactly what that means for the believer. In what way are we to become "like Christ"?

Beginning in 1993, I began serving at a church in Austin, Texas as Pastor of College Ministries. Over the next 10 years, the university student population in our church grew to more than 1000 students. We had a full-time staff of seven workers and a volunteer leadership

| BELONG | | | BECOME | | BEYOND | | |
|---|---|---|---|---|---|---|---|
| TO CHRIST | TO COMMUNITY | TO CHURCH | INCIDENTAL TRANSFORMATION | INTENTIONAL TRANSFORMATION | INTO MY CHURCH | INTO MY NEIGHBORHOOD | INTO MY WORLD |

team of many more. At one point, we had more than 100 discipleship groups meeting, studying God's Word and growing in godliness.

As it was, we typically had a student attend our ministry for an average of three years. Upon graduation, many moved out of town and a new group of students would arrive. We knew that we only had three years to "make disciples"—about the same length of time Jesus spent with His followers. This meant that we had to prioritize which spiritual life lessons were most essential for the growing Christian. As each of us determines to walk with Jesus, we must ask, "What are the most important biblical principles we should learn for the greatest life transformation?" Not to exclude all other spiritual truth, but what are the fundamentals of the spiritual life? Our ministry team focused on four areas of development: Vision, Knowledge, Character and Skills.

## Vision

Vision is what a disciple "sees." Aristotle described vision as a picture in the soul of a person. In his book *Visioneering*, pastor Andy Stanley writes, "Vision is the clear mental picture of what could be, fueled by the conviction that it should be." It is the compelling dream or desire set before an individual which drives them day by day.

In the early 1900s, the Wright brothers' vision of flight pushed them to get the first airplane off the ground. Apple innovator Steve Jobs' vision of "a computer in every home" produced a whole movement of technology which has since changed the world. African-American Rosa Parks' refusal to give up her seat on a bus in 1955 was fueled by a personal vision of desegregation and equal opportunity for all people.

Visionaries see a preferred future with their "mind's eye." That is, they may not be able to actually see or touch or realize the results of their actions *yet*, but they possess a firm conviction that their decisions will produce the desired outcome. When Jesus said, *"Do you not say, 'Four months more and then the harvest'? I tell you, open your eyes and look at the fields! They are ripe for harvest"* (John 4:35), He was urging His followers to imagine the evangelistic fruit which was not yet, but could be if more workers went "into the harvest."

A person's vision is what energizes everything they do. If a person has a vision of being rich and successful, every decision they make—from college courses to the clothes they wear to their first interview—will be calculated in regards to its rich and successful benefits. Someone who has a vision of becoming a great athlete will adopt a rigorous exercise schedule and dietary plan to achieve that goal. In fact, *every* person has a vision of something. It may not be a consciously-formed vision or carved into a monument, but the passions and priorities of each person's life will express to their vision.

So it is important for the disciple of Jesus to not only have vision, but to have the *right* vision. Proverbs 29:18 states, *"Where there is no vision, the people perish."* The vision mentioned in this verse isn't *any* vision, but a biblical one. And, if God's people lack a godly vision, they will never end up where God wants them to be.

Think of Jesus' final words on the cross. In His last breaths, He gasped, *"It is finished!"* (John 19:30) and died. What a declaration—to come to the end of your life and have confidence that your mission is complete and that your vision has been realized. A few chapters earlier, Jesus prayed, *"I have brought you glory on earth by completing the work you gave me to do"* (John 17:4). From the moment He was born, Jesus saw the end and directed every part of His life to fulfilling that vision.

Instead of announcing "It is finished!" at the end of their lives, far too many Christians will wonder "Is it finished?" because they have not looked at life through the eyes of God. As a result, they succeeded in a vision that was self-serving, godless and fruitless, lacking any eternal benefit. Of course, such "success" is no success at all.

What we have concluded is that the disciple's vision for their life must be God's vision for their life. And, God's overarching vision for us is the same as God's vision for God. What God wants for me is what God wants for Himself *through me.* So before trying to figure out some nuanced vision for my life, unique from all other people, I must understand what God's vision is for God and then set my sights on that vision for my life in whatever God calls me to do.

We discover God's great vision by understanding the overarching theme of the Bible: God's glorification of Himself through the redemption of sinners. God intends to glorify Himself—to magnify His supremacy in all things. He alone is worthy to be exalted as the true God (Revelation 4:11) and will not "share His glory" with anyone or anything else (Isaiah 42:8, 48:11).

God glorifies Himself through "reflecting" and "reigning." First, He created the world to reflect His glorious power, sustenance and beauty (Psalm 19:1, Romans 1:20). Human beings, made in God's image, were created for His glory (Isaiah 43:7). Second, He created the world and people as a kingdom where He would rule as our rightful and only King (Psalm 46:10). As people multiplied and lived under God's reign, His kingdom would grow and God would be further glorified. In this way, the expansion of God's Kingdom made possible the glorification of God.

Unfortunately, sin contaminated God's glorious reflection in humanity and violated God's rightful rule in the world as Satan attempted to assert his own authority and lead people into rebellion. So, to recover His glory, God chose to redeem human beings through the death of His Son, Jesus. He saves and sanctifies people to restore His glory (Psalm 79:9, 2 Corinthians 3:18, Ephesians 1:3-14). *"For God, who said, 'Let light shine out of darkness,' made his light shine in our hearts to give us the light of the knowledge of the glory of God in the face of Christ"* (2 Corinthians 4:6). God's goal is for His glory to shine through His people and throughout the earth.

So, the Christian's vision must be centered on magnification and mission—to see the glory of God manifested through the redemption of people everywhere. In Matthew 6:33, Jesus said, *"But seek first his kingdom and his righteousness, and all these things will be given to you as well."* Set your sights on who God is and His reign over all, and everything else will follow. If the disciple desires and delights in the glory of God and the establishment of His reign among all people, this vision will shape the rest of their spiritual journey.

## Knowledge

Knowledge is what a disciple understands to be true. Before belonging to Jesus Christ, people neither seek truth nor understand truth (Romans 3:11). Because they do not possess the Holy Spirit, they cannot understand spiritual things (1 Corinthians 2:14). The Bible describes this condition as "foolishness"—being dull to the wisdom and ways of God. In fact, the fool denies the existence of God, despises correction, hates instruction, is impulsive in passions and decisions, speaks proudly and is bent on destruction (Psalm 14:1-2).

However, when a person turns to the Lord, He gives them His Holy Spirit who, in turn, gives them the "mind of Christ" (1 Corinthians 2:12, 16). With this new spiritual disposition, the Christian is able to "grow in the knowledge of the Lord," increasing understanding of God and His ways (Colossians 1:10, 2 Peter 3:18). Though the accumulation of knowledge may be nothing more than the mere *appearance of maturity* for some people (1 Corinthians 8:1), for the truly mature it is the foundation for their spiritual zeal (Proverbs 19:2, Romans 10:1-3). As they read God's Word, they desire, understand and apply spiritual truth that sets them free (John 8:32).

The Bible, in its 66 books, is filled with life-changing truth. But in a limited discipleship relationship, there are some truths that must take priority for the growing believer. At Pantego Bible Church, we refer to Core Beliefs—essential truths that every Christian must understand. Many of these competencies were originally proposed in *The Connecting Church*, by Pastor Randy Frazee. I suggest a modified list here:

**Authority of the Bible** — The disciple knows that God has specially revealed Himself through His inspired Word and that the Bible has the right to direct a person's beliefs and actions.

*For the word of God is living and active. Sharper than any double-edged sword, it penetrates even to dividing soul and spirit, joints and marrow; it judges the thoughts and attitudes of the heart. Nothing in all creation is hidden from God's sight. Everything is uncovered and laid bare before the eyes of him to whom we must give account.* (Hebrews 4:12-13)

*Every word of God is flawless; he is a shield to those who take refuge in him. Do not add to his words, or he will rebuke you and prove you a liar.* (Proverbs 30:5-6)

**The Church** — The disciple knows that the church is the assembly of the saints who gather in community, are equipped for ministry and are sent into the world with a mission to make God known.

*For we were all baptized by one Spirit into one body—Whether Jews or Greeks, slave or free—we were all given the one Spirit to drink.* (1 Corinthians 12:13)

*But you are a chosen people, a royal priesthood, a holy nation, God's special possession, that you may declare the praises of him who called you out of darkness into his wonderful light.* (1 Peter 2:9)

**Eternity** — The disciple knows that all people are immortal and will spend eternity either in the blessed presence of God or forever separated from Him.

*Just as man is destined to die once, and after that to face judgment...* (Hebrews 9:27)

*But Christ has indeed been raised from the dead, the firstfruits of those who have fallen asleep. For since death came through a man, the resurrection of the dead comes also through a man. For as in Adam all die, so in Christ all will be made alive. But each in his own turn: Christ, the firstfruits; then, when he comes, those who belong to him.* (1 Corinthians 15:20-23)

*"Then he will say to those on his left, 'Depart from me, you who are cursed, into the eternal fire prepared for the devil and his angels.... Then they will go away to eternal punishment, but the righteous to eternal life."* (Matthew 25:41, 46)

**Holy Spirit** — The disciple knows the person and work of the Holy Spirit, especially in regards to His ministry of conviction, calling, conversion and changing people.

*I will give you a new heart and put a new spirit in you; I will remove from you your heart of stone and give you a heart of flesh. And I will put my Spirit in you and move you to follow my decrees and be careful to keep my laws.* (Ezekiel 36:26-27)

*"But you will receive power when the Holy Spirit comes on you; and you will be my witnesses in Jerusalem, and in all Judea and Samaria, and to the ends of the earth."* (Acts 1:8)

*You, however, are controlled not by the sinful nature but by the Spirit, if the Spirit of God lives in you. And if anyone does not have the Spirit of Christ, he does not belong to Christ.* (Romans 8:9)

**Humanity** — The disciple knows the value of all people, their moral condition that separates them from God and the universal need for rescue made possible only through God's Son.

*So God created man in his own image, in the image of God he created him; male and female he created them.* (Genesis 1:27)

*For you formed my inward parts; you knitted me together in my mother's womb. I praise you, for I am fearfully and wonderfully made.* (Psalm 139:13)

*...for all have sinned and fall short of the glory of God...*(Romans 3:23)

**Identity in Christ** — The disciple knows their new position as a child of God and learns to confidently and humbly live out of this position, resisting the lies of the devil and being fully assured of their salvation.

*How great is the love the Father has lavished on us, that we should be called children of God! And that is what we are!* (1 John 3:1)

*I have been crucified with Christ and I no longer live, but Christ lives in me. The life I live in the body, I live by faith in the Son of God, who loved me and gave himself for me.* (Galatians 2:20)

*Since, then, you have been raised with Christ, set your hearts on things above, where Christ is seated at the right hand of God. Set your minds on things above, not on earthly things. For you died, and your life is now hidden with Christ in God. When Christ, who is your life, appears, then you also will appear with him in glory.* (Colossians 3:1-4)

**Jesus Christ** — The disciple knows the person and work of Jesus, including His incarnation, death on the cross and resurrection from the dead.

*In the beginning was the Word, and the Word was with God, and the Word was God. He was with God in the beginning. Through him all things were made; without him nothing was made that has been made. In him was life, and that life was the light of men.* (John 1:1-4)

*In the past God spoke to our forefathers through the prophets at many times and in various ways, but in these last days he has spoken to us by his Son, whom he appointed heir of all things, and through whom he made the universe. The Son is the radiance of God's glory and the exact representation of his being, sustaining all things by his powerful word. After he had provided purification for sins, he sat down at the right hand of the Majesty in heaven. So he became as much superior to the angels as the name he has inherited is superior to theirs.* (Hebrews 1:1-4)

*But you are a chosen people, a royal priesthood, a holy nation, God's special possession, that you may declare the praises of him who called you out of darkness into his wonderful light.* (1 Peter 2:9)

**Life Purpose** — The disciple knows that they are a steward of God's resources and have been redeemed to participate in God's Kingdom purposes for God's glory.

*However, I consider my life worth nothing to me, if only I may finish the race and complete the task the Lord Jesus has given me—the task of testifying to the gospel of God's grace.* (Acts 20:24)

*Now I rejoice in what was suffered for you, and I fill up in my flesh what is still lacking in regard to Christ's afflictions, for the sake of his body, which is the church. I have become its servant by the commission God gave me to present to you the word of God in its fullness—the mystery that has been kept hidden for ages and generations, but is now disclosed to the saints. To them God has chosen to make known among the Gentiles the glorious riches of this mystery, which is Christ in you, the hope of glory.* (Colossians 1:24-27)

**Personal God** — The disciple knows that God exists; what God is like, including an appreciation of the Trinity; and that God's purpose is to glorify Himself and build His kingdom.

*"The God who made the world and everything in it is the Lord of heaven and earth and does not live in temples built by hands. And he is not served by human hands, as if he needed anything, because he himself gives all men life and breath and everything else. From one man he made every nation of men, that they should inhabit the whole earth; and he determined the times set for them and the exact places where they should live. God did this so that men would seek him and perhaps reach out for him and find him, though he is not far from each one of us. 'For in him we live and move and have our being.'"* (Acts 17:24-28)

*Hear, O Israel: The LORD our God, the LORD is one.* (Deuteronomy 6:4)

**Salvation** — The disciple knows that people come into a right relationship with God by grace through faith in His Son, Jesus.

*"For God so loved the world that he gave his one and only Son, that whoever believes in him shall not perish but have eternal life." (John 3:16)*

*Jesus answered, "I am the way and the truth and the life. No one comes to the Father except through me." (John 14:6)*

*But these are written that you may believe that Jesus is the Christ, the Son of God, and that by believing you may have life in his name. (John 20:31)*

*For it is by grace you have been saved, through faith—and this not from yourselves, it is the gift of God—not by works, so that no one can boast.* (Ephesians 2:8-9)

## Character

Character is what a disciple becomes. It refers to the inner virtues cultivated by the Holy Spirit. As a believer is conformed to the image of Jesus, they think and talk and act like Jesus—the proof of a heart increasingly transformed. Peter describes this change in 2 Peter 1:3-8,

*His divine power has given us everything we need for life and godliness through our knowledge of him who called us by his own glory and goodness. Through these he has given us his very great and precious promises, so that through them you may participate in the divine nature and escape the corruption in the world caused by evil desires. For this very reason, make every effort to add to your faith goodness; and to goodness, knowledge; and to knowledge, self-control; and to self-control, perseverance; and to perseverance, godliness; and to godliness, brotherly kindness; and to brotherly kindness, love. For if you possess these qualities in increasing measure, they will keep you from being ineffective and unproductive in your knowledge of our Lord Jesus Christ.*

Several spiritual principles are stated in this powerful passage. First, God, through His Spirit, has provided every Christian what we need to live a godly life. Second, according to the promise of God, we are able to "participate in the divine nature"—becoming like Jesus—and escape the corruption of the world (see also Romans 12:1-2). Third, since we have this potential, we should intentionally "add to" our faith all of the virtues mentioned. Finally, as our character is conformed to Christ, we become productive and effective in our life with Jesus.

Character is essentially the "overflow of the heart." The Christian wants to be loving, gracious, merciful and kind at the core. But, even before the believer experiences this inward change, they can *choose* to act according to these and other character traits. Very often, the Bible commands the Christian to show love, be gracious, act mercifully or treat people with kindness, with the expectation that as they cooperate with the Holy Spirit, they will learn to *be* what they do. In other words, their actions will form their character.

Like knowledge, there are dozens of character traits that God wishes to refine in the Christian. The following 11 Core Character Traits are especially important:

**Love** — The disciple demonstrates unconditional, unlimited and unselfish love for others.

*Dear friends, let us love one another, for love comes from God. Everyone who loves has been born of God and knows God. Whoever does not love does not know God, because God is love. This is how God showed his love among us: He sent his one and only Son into the world that we might live through him. This is love: not that we loved God, but that he loved us and sent his Son as an atoning sacrifice for our sins. Dear friends, since God so loved us, we also ought to love one another. No one has ever seen God; but if we love one another, God lives in us and his love is made complete in us.* (1 John 4:7 -12)

**Joy** — The disciple demonstrates God-centered gladness in spite of their circumstances.

*Consider it pure joy, my brothers, whenever you face trials of many kinds, because you know that the testing of your faith develops perseverance.* (James 1:2-3)

*Though you have not seen him, you love him; and even though you do not see him now, you believe in him and are filled with an inexpressible and glorious joy, for you are receiving the goal of your faith, the salvation of your souls.* (1 Peter 1:8-9)

**Peace** — The disciple demonstrates contentment in life because they are rightly related to God and seeks to be rightly related to others.

*Therefore, since we have been justified through faith, we have peace with God through our Lord Jesus Christ, through whom we have gained access by faith into this grace in which we now stand.* (Romans 5:1-2)

*Do not repay anyone evil for evil. Be careful to do what is right in the eyes of everybody. If it is possible, as far as it depends on you, live at peace with everyone.* (Romans 12:17-18)

*Blessed are the peacemakers, for they will be called sons of God.* (Matthew 5:9)

**Patience** — The disciple demonstrates endurance in the unavoidable pressures of life.

*Be still before the LORD and wait patiently for him; do not fret when men succeed in their ways, when they carry out their wicked schemes.* (Psalm 37:7)

*Be joyful in hope, patient in affliction, faithful in prayer.* (Romans 12:12)

*For it is commendable if a man bears up under the pain of unjust suffering because he is conscious of God. But how is it to your credit if you receive a beating for doing wrong and endure it? But if you suffer for doing good and you endure it, this is commendable before God. To this you were called, because Christ suffered for you, leaving you an example, that you should follow in his steps.* (1 Peter 2:19-21)

**Kindness/Goodness** — The disciple demonstrates favor toward people by doing and saying things that bless others.

*Therefore, as God's chosen people, holy and dearly loved, clothe yourselves with compassion, kindness, humility, gentleness and patience.* (Colossians 3:12)

*But the fruit of the Spirit is love, joy, peace, patience, kindness, goodness, faithfulness, gentleness and self-control.* (Galatians 5:22-23)

*So then, as we have opportunity, let us do good to everyone, and especially to those who are of the household of faith.* (Galatians 6:10)

**Faithfulness** — The disciple demonstrates dependable loyalty toward God and others in the commitments they have made.

*Whoever can be trusted with very little can also be trusted with much, and whoever is dishonest with very little will also be dishonest with much.* (Luke 16:10)

*But be sure to fear the LORD and serve him faithfully with all your heart; consider what great things he has done for you.* (1 Samuel 12:24)

**Gentleness** — The disciple demonstrates a calm spirit of thoughtfulness when dealing with others.

*A gentle answer turns away wrath, but a harsh word stirs up anger.* (Proverbs 15:1)

*Rejoice in the Lord always. I will say it again: Rejoice! Let your gentleness be evident to all. The Lord is near.* (Philippians 4:4-5)

*Blessed are the meek, for they will inherit the earth.* (Matthew 5:5)

**Self-Control** — The disciple demonstrates temperance in their speech, attitudes and actions.

*For the grace of God that brings salvation has appeared to all men. It teaches us to say "No" to ungodliness and worldly passions, and to live self-controlled, upright and godly lives in this present age, while we wait for the blessed hope—the glorious appearing of our great God and Savior, Jesus Christ, who gave himself for us to redeem us from all wickedness and to purify for himself a people that are his very own, eager to do what is good.* (Titus 2:11-14)

*Be self-controlled and alert. Your enemy the devil prowls around like a roaring lion looking for someone to devour.* (1 Peter 5:8)

**Grace** — The disciple demonstrates forgiveness, mercy and generosity to others, even those who have offended them.

*Freely you have received, freely give.* (Matthew 10:8)

*Bear with each other and forgive whatever grievances you may have against one another. Forgive as the Lord forgave you.* (Colossians 3:13)

*Let your conversation be always full of grace, seasoned with salt, so that you may know how to answer everyone.* (Colossians 4:6)

**Hope** — The disciple demonstrates a growing anticipation of God's future promises and their secure eternity with Him.

*Praise be to the God and Father of our Lord Jesus Christ! In his great mercy he has given us new birth into a living hope through the resurrection of Jesus Christ from the dead, 4 and into an inheritance that can never perish, spoil or fade—kept in heaven for you, 5 who through faith are shielded by God's power until the coming of the salvation that is ready to be revealed in the last time.* (1 Peter 1:3-5)

*May the God of hope fill you with all joy and peace as you trust in him, so that you may overflow with hope by the power of the Holy Spirit.* (Romans 15:13)

*But now, Lord, what do I look for? My hope is in you.* (Psalm 39:7)

**Humility** — The disciple esteems others above themselves through service and deference.

*Do nothing out of selfish ambition or vain conceit, but in humility consider others better than yourselves. Each of you should look not only to your own interests, but also to the interests of others. Your attitude should be the same as that of Christ Jesus.* (Philippians 2:3-5)

*Be completely humble and gentle; be patient, bearing with one another in love.* (Ephesians 4:2)

## Skills

Skills are what a disciple can do. These are the practices or aptitudes of the spiritual life. Just as a child learns how to walk, ride a bike or drive a car with age, so the Christian develops skills that help their spiritual growth and make them more fruitful in their service to God. Historically, many skills have been called "disciplines" of the spiritual life. As opposed to "works" which people do to gain favor with God, disciplines are healthy spiritual habits inspired by grace. They are practices which overflow from a person's relationship with God.

Just as the vision, knowledge and character mentioned above are normative for the Christian, so these skills should be normative as well. If I were invited to someone's home for a meal and they were feeding their 13-year-old son, I would form one of two conclusions: Their son was lazy or their son had a developmental difficulty that prevented him from being able to feed himself. Similarly, we must conclude that Christians who do not pray, share their faith or practice financial stewardship, for example, are either lazy or spiritually deficient. A growing disciple becomes increasingly proficient at spiritual skills.

Similar to the other competencies, there are dozens of skills that God wishes to develop in the Christian. The following 10 Core Skills are especially important:

**Bible Study** — The disciple studies God's Word, seeking to understand spiritual truth as an authoritative guide for their life.

*All Scripture is God-breathed and is useful for teaching, rebuking, correcting and training in righteousness, so that the man of God may be thoroughly equipped for every good work.* (2 Timothy 3:16-17)

*Open my eyes that I may see wonderful things in your law.* (Psalm 119:18)

*Do not let this Book of the Law depart from your mouth; meditate on it day and night, so that you may be careful to do everything written in it. Then you will be prosperous and successful.* (Joshua 1:8)

**Biblical Community** — The disciple meets regularly with other Christians for mutual encouragement, accountability and ministry. A commitment to community also means that the disciple actively seeks reconciliation.

*Just as each of us has one body with many members, and these members do not all have the same function, so in Christ we who are many form one body, and each member belongs to all the others.* (Romans 12:4-5)

*Carry each other's burdens, and in this way you will fulfill the law of Christ.* (Galatians 6:2)

*And let us consider how we may spur one another on toward love and good deeds. Let us not give up meeting together, as some are in the habit of doing, but let us encourage one another—and all the more as you see the Day approaching.* (Hebrews 10:24-25)

**Compassion** — The disciple seeks to serve the last, the least and the lost in their community by meeting needs with time and resources.

*Praise be to the God and Father of our Lord Jesus Christ, the Father of compassion and the God of all comfort, who comforts us in all our troubles, so that we can comfort those in any trouble with the comfort we ourselves have received from God.* (2 Corinthians 1:3-4)

*Religion that God our Father accepts as pure and faultless is this: to look after orphans and widows in their distress and to keep oneself from being polluted by the world.* (James 1:27)

**Disciple-making** — The disciple intentionally seeks to multiply their vision, knowledge, character and skills in others to help them in their spiritual journeys.

*All authority in heaven and on earth has been given to me. Therefore go and make disciples of all nations, baptizing them in the name of the Father and of the Son and of the Holy Spirit, and teaching them to obey everything I have commanded you. And surely I am with you always, to the very end of the age.* (Matthew 28:18-20)

*You did not choose me, but I chose you and appointed you to go and bear fruit—fruit that will last.* (John 15:16)

*And the things you have heard me say in the presence of many witnesses entrust to reliable men who will also be qualified to teach others.* (2 Timothy 2:2)

**Evangelism** — The disciple can articulate their salvation story and shares the Gospel of Jesus through personal demonstration and proclamation, both in their neighborhood and around the world.

*You are the light of the world. A city on a hill cannot be hidden.* ¹⁵ *Neither do people light a lamp and put it under a bowl. Instead they put it on its stand, and it gives light to everyone in the house. In the same way, let your light shine before men, that they may see your good deeds and praise your Father in heaven.* (Matthew 5:14-16)

*But you will receive power when the Holy Spirit comes on you; and you will be my witnesses in Jerusalem, and in all Judea and Samaria, and to the ends of the earth.* (Acts 1:8)

*I have made you a light for the Gentiles, that you may bring salvation to the ends of the earth.* (Acts 13:47)

**Generosity** — The disciple gladly and generously gives their resources to expand God's Kingdom through their church and beyond.

*Give, and it will be given to you. A good measure, pressed down, shaken together and running over, will be poured into your lap. For with the measure you use, it will be measured to you.* (Luke 6:38)

*From everyone who has been given much, much will be demanded; and from the one who has been entrusted with much, much more will be asked.* (Luke 12:48)

*Whoever sows sparingly will also reap sparingly, and whoever sows generously will also reap generously. Each man should give what he has decided in his heart to give, not reluctantly or under compulsion, for God loves a cheerful giver. And God is able to make all grace abound to you, so that in all things at all times, having all that you need, you will abound in every good work. As it is written: "He has scattered abroad his gifts to the poor; his righteousness endures forever." Now he who supplies seed to the sower and bread for food will also supply and increase your store of seed and will enlarge the harvest of your righteousness. You will be made rich in every way so that you can be generous on every occasion, and through us your generosity will result in thanksgiving to God.* (2 Corinthians 9:6-11)

**Prayer** — The disciple seeks God in prayer, confessing sin, declaring God's praises, showing gratitude for God's blessings and trusting God for His will for themselves and others.

*The LORD is near to all who call on him, to all who call on him in truth.* (Psalm 145:18)

*Do not be anxious about anything, but in everything, by prayer and petition, with thanksgiving, present your requests to God. And the peace of God, which transcends all understanding, will guard your hearts and your minds in Christ Jesus.* (Philippians 4:6-7)

*If we confess our sins, he is faithful and just and will forgive us our sins and purify us from all unrighteousness.* (1 John 1:9)

**Single-mindedness** — The disciple practices simplicity of life in order to focus on God's priorities for their life and others.

*I seek you with all my heart; do not let me stray from your commands.* (Psalm 119:10)

*But seek first his kingdom and his righteousness, and all these things will be given to you as well.* (Matthew 6:33)

*Therefore, since we are surrounded by such a great cloud of witnesses, let us throw off everything that hinders and the sin that so easily entangles, and let us run with perseverance the race marked out for us. Let us fix our eyes on Jesus, the author and perfecter of our faith, who for the joy set before him endured the cross, scorning its shame, and sat down at the right hand of the throne of God. Consider him who endured such opposition from sinful men, so that you will not grow weary and lose heart.* (Hebrews 12:1-3)

**Spiritual Gifts** — The disciple serves their church through the exercise of their spiritual gift(s).

*The greatest among you will be your servant. For whoever exalts himself will be humbled, and whoever humbles himself will be exalted.* (Matthew 23:11-12)

*Each one should use whatever gift he has received to serve others, faithfully administering God's grace in its various forms.* (1 Peter 4:10)

*Your attitude should be the same as that of Christ Jesus: Who, being in very nature God, did not consider equality with God something to be grasped, but made himself nothing, taking the very nature of a servant, being made in human likeness.* (Philippians 2:5-7)

*Now to each one the manifestation of the Spirit is given for the common good.* (1 Corinthians 12:7)

**Worship** — The disciple exalts God, both privately and publically, for who God is and what God has done.

*My mouth is filled with your praise, declaring your splendor all day long.* (Psalm 71:8)

*Give thanks to the LORD, call on his name; make known among the nations what he has done. Sing to him, sing praise to him; tell of all his wonderful acts. Glory in his holy name; let the hearts of those who seek the LORD rejoice. Look to the LORD and his strength; seek his face always.* (Psalm 105:1-4)

*Do you not know that your body is a temple of the Holy Spirit, who is in you, whom you have received from God? You are not your own; you were bought at a price. Therefore honor God with your body* (1 Corinthians 6:19 -20)

*So whether you eat or drink or whatever you do, do it all for the glory of God.* (1 Corinthians 10:31)

*Dear children, keep yourselves from idols.* (1 John 5:21)

No doubt, the reader will ask, "But, what about _____?" and will wonder about some foundational truth, some character trait, or some skill not mention in these lists. Where is the imminent return of Jesus, or faith, or fasting? Remember that none of the lists are intended to be exhaustive. They are foundational. More important is that the disciple *has* a list—a core set of essential truths which become the focus of their spiritual development.

## SUMMARY

In this final chapter about spiritual transformation, we have learned about vital dimensions of discipleship. Vision is what disciples "see," knowledge is what they know, character is who they are and skills are what they can do. Each is important for the formation of fully devoted followers of Jesus Christ. The disciple wishing to grow in their life with Jesus will welcome this holistic transformation.

## TAKE THE NEXT STEP

1. In your own words, describe God's central vision for your life.

2. Without looking back through this chapter, identify 10 core truths (knowledge) you think are essential for every disciple. Next, compare your list with the list in this book. What changes might you make to either list?

3. Without looking back through this chapter, identify 10 core character traits you think are essential for every disciple. Next, compare your list with the list in this book. What changes might you make to either list?

4. Without looking back through this chapter, identify 10 core skills you think are essential for every disciple. Next, compare your list with the list in this book. What changes might you make to either list?

5. What is the most important thing you learned from this chapter?

# BEYOND: INTO MY CHURCH

*There is a church because there is a mission, not vice versa.*
David Bosch

In 1999, two researchers at Harvard University conducted a humorous experiment to explore people's attention to details. For the experiment, participants were invited to watch a video of six players passing a ball between them. Three players wore black shirts and the other three wore white ones. The study participant was instructed to count the number of times that players on the white-shirt team passed the ball while ignoring passes made by those wearing black shirts. About 30 seconds into the video, while the players shuffled about the room, passing the ball, a person dressed in a gorilla costume entered the scene, walked among the players and exited. The video continued for another 30 seconds and, afterward, study participants were asked how many passes were made. Next, they were asked if they saw the gorilla. Remarkably, only 48% of people noticed the gorilla in the video!

The experiment was designed to explore the theory of "inattentional blindness" or "selective focus," where people often

| BELONG | | | BECOME | | BEYOND | | |
|---|---|---|---|---|---|---|---|
| TO CHRIST | TO COMMUNITY | TO CHURCH | INCIDENTAL TRANSFORMATION | INTENTIONAL TRANSFORMATION | INTO MY CHURCH | INTO MY NEIGHBORHOOD | INTO MY WORLD |

miss the most important thing while concentrating on less significant details. This is a common problem among Christians. Churches focus on helping people connect with God and others (BELONG) and emphasize spiritual growth (BECOME), but they often stop short of the most significant goal: to mobilize disciples for mission (BEYOND).

If you are a pastor reading this book, this is a good time to pause and ask yourself the questions, "What is the purpose of my church? Why do I do what I do? Have I been focusing on the right thing or has my attention to some things caused me to lose focus on the larger goal of the church?" Not just pastors, but every attendee should ask the same questions.

To understand the mission of the church, we must understand the mission of God. In Genesis 1 and 2, God created the world and people for His glory (see Psalm 19:1 and Isaiah 43:7). That is, everything was created to make much of the magnificence of its Creator. However, in Genesis 3, sin corrupted the world and turned God-centered people into self-centered rebels. The rest of history is God's reclamation of His glory through the redemption of sinners.

Genesis 12:1-3 is a significant text in salvation history. God called Abram (an act of Divine grace) to be the father of the Jewish people and promised his people land, spiritual blessings and innumerable descendants. Unfortunately, many ancient Jews and modern readers interpret God's promises to Abram to be exclusive, as if God's blessings were intended for only one group of people. However, God concludes His covenant, *"all peoples on earth will be blessed through you."* The Jews were blessed to be a blessing.

With a similar theme, Psalm 67 highlights God's missional purposes. In verse 1, the psalmist prays, *"May God be gracious to us and bless us and make his face shine upon us."* Reflecting the priestly blessing (Numbers 6:24-26), this verse requests that God shower His kindness upon His people. But God's blessings to people are never meant to end with people. Rather, His blessings pass through people to others so that others may experience the goodness of God. Verse 2 highlights this goal: *"that your ways may be known on earth, your salvation among all nations."*

This "blessed-to-be-a-blessing" principle is frequently repeated in the New Testament:

*"You are the light of the world. A town built on a hill cannot be hidden. Neither do people light a lamp and put it under a bowl. Instead they put it on its stand, and it gives light to everyone in the house. In the same way, let your light shine before others, that they may see your good deeds and glorify your Father in heaven."* (Matthew 5:14-16)

*Go rather to the lost sheep of Israel. As you go, preach this message: 'The kingdom of heaven is near.' Heal the sick, raise the dead, cleanse those who have leprosy, drive out demons. Freely you have received, freely give.* (Matthew 10:6-8)

*Jesus said, "Peace be with you! As the Father has sent me, I am sending you."* (John 20:21)

*Praise be to the God and Father of our Lord Jesus Christ, the Father of compassion and the God of all comfort, who comforts us in all our troubles, so that we can comfort those in any trouble with the comfort we ourselves have received from God.* (2 Corinthians 1:3-4)

*Now I rejoice in what I am suffering for you, and I fill up in my flesh what is still lacking in regard to Christ's afflictions, for the sake of his body, which is the church.* (Colossians 1:24)

*You are a chosen people, a royal priesthood, a holy nation, a people belonging to God, that you may declare the praises of him who called you out of darkness into his wonderful light.* (1 Peter 2:9)

This pay-it-forward principle is clear. Those who have been enlightened, shine brightly among others. Those who have received, give. Those who have been comforted, comfort others. Those who enjoy peace, announce peace. This is the mission of the church: to extend the blessings of God into the world so that the world may come to know God and worship God. Alan Hirsch, in *Forgotten Ways*, writes,

When the church is on mission, it is the true church. The church itself is not only a product of that mission but is obligated and destined to extend it by whatever means possible.

The mission of God flows directly through every believer and every community of faith that adheres to Jesus. (p. 82)

Similarly, in his excellent book titled *The New Testament Order for Church and Missionary*, A.R. Hay rightly observes,

The Lord founded the church as a missionary organization. It was not an ecclesiastical organization with missionary endeavor as a department of its work. Missionaries were its leaders. Its primary purpose was missionary and all its members engaged in the propagation of the gospel. (p. 131)

When I arrived at Pantego Bible Church in 2005, I found a church that understood the first step in the spiritual pathway: BELONG. Our church set the standard for biblical community, with many of its members growing in relationship with God and each other. But, while our communities were encouraged to participate in local and global outreach, the church had virtually no culture of mission. The church was inwardly focused but lacking external impact.

During that time, I was midway through my graduate studies in seminary and was reading several books on the purpose of the church. One book, *The Continuing Conversion of the Church*, was especially helpful. Author Darrell Guder notes that for most churches, the end of discipleship is discipleship. That is, most churches have a church-centric goal of making their own people *better*. But, God's end for discipleship has always been mission. God changes people to change their world. Expanding a definition borrowed from another missional writer, David Bosch, Guder states,

Mission (may be understood) as being derived from the very nature of God. It (is) thus put into the context of the doctrine of the Trinity, not of ecclesiology or soteriology. The classical doctrine of the mission Dei as God the Father sending the Son, and God the Father and the Son sending the Spirit (is) expanded to include yet another "movement": Father, Son, and Holy Spirit sending the church into the world....mission is not primarily an activity of the church, but an attribute of God...Mission is thereby seen as a movement from God to the world: the church is viewed as an instrument of that mission...There is church because there is mission, not vice versa. (p. 20)

Those who BELONG to Jesus and BECOME more like Jesus go BEYOND to take Jesus into their world. "'*Come, follow me,*' *Jesus said,* '*and I will make you fishers of men*'" (Matthew 4:19). This is God's goal for every Christian. This is His goal for every church. The church is God's instrument of redemption in the world. We must never so focus on community and transformation that we lose sight of this biblical mission.

## Into the Church

When Peter preached his first sermon at Pentecost, "*three thousand were added to their number that day*" (Acts 2:41). As the community of believers grew more connected, "*the Lord added to their number daily those who were being saved*" (Acts 2:47). As the church expanded and began to move into the world, manifesting the power of God and preaching the Gospel, "*many who heard the message believed, and the number of men grew to about five thousand*" (Acts 4:4). As we grow disciples, we grow churches.

But, when churches grow, the needs within churches increase. As the Jerusalem church added to their numbers, "*the Grecian Jews among them complained against the Hebraic Jews because their widows were being overlooked in the daily distribution of food*" (Acts 6:1). Up to this point, the Apostles were able to manage all the ministry themselves. But now, more servants were required to ensure the continuing success of the church. So, the leaders directed the people to "*choose seven men from among you who are full of the Spirit*" (6:3). People were the answer.

It is significant that the primary requirement for these additional servants is that they be full of the Holy Spirit. The reason is because the Spirit forms character and those who serve in the church must, first and foremost, be men and women of character. Serving the church requires humility, generosity and compassion—all virtues of the Spirit (see Philippians 2:1-4). God prioritizes character over competency when appointing servants in the local church.

Another reason why the Spirit is so essential is because the Holy Spirit equips people for service. The Apostles explained that it would not be good for them to neglect their ministry of preaching the word to wait on tables. It wasn't that their responsibility was superior, but that they had been equipped for one kind of service, and the care of widows required servants equipped for that particular task. The Holy Spirit gives gifts to His people and then gives His people to one another.

A right understanding of spiritual gifts enables believers to go BEYOND into their church. The Bible teaches several fundamental truths about spiritual gifts:

**Every Christian has at least one spiritual gift.** Paul writes, *"Now to each one the manifestation of the Spirit is given for the common good"* (1 Corinthians 12:7) and *"to each one of us grace has been given as Christ apportioned it"* (Ephesians 4:7). Not only pastors, but all Christians have received at least one spiritual gift.

**Spiritual gifts are given according the will of the Holy Spirit.** No one earns or learns a spiritual gift. Rather, *"but one and the same Spirit works all these things distributing to each one individually as He wills"* (1 Corinthians 12:11). Spiritual gifts are manifestations of God's grace, given freely and without condition. A Christian may desire a gift (1 Corinthians 14:1), but that is no guarantee that the gift will be given.

**Each Christian has a responsibility to use their gift.** Peter commands, *"As each one has received a gift, minister in it to one another, as good stewards of the manifold grace of God"* (1 Peter 4:10). Likewise, Paul urges his young disciple, Timothy, *"Do not neglect the gift that was given you"* (1 Timothy 4:14). Gifts are not given to be stored, but to be used.

Do not forget the Parable of the Talents where a master left his stewards in charge of his resources (Matthew 25:14-30). One servant squandered what had been entrusted to them, but one proved to be faithful. That one, not the lazy one, was later entrusted with more responsibility and enjoyed the happiness of his master.

**Spiritual gifts are intended to be given away.** God gives gifts to His people and then He gives people to His church to accomplish the mission of the church. The gifts He gives are not for the recipient but intended for the Body. We see this principle at work in one of the most extensive passages on spiritual gifts in Ephesians 4:11-16. The Apostle Paul instructs the church:

> *It was he who gave some to be apostles, some to be prophets, some to be evangelists, and some to be pastors and teachers, to prepare God's people for works of service, so that the body of Christ may be built up until we all reach unity in the faith and in the knowledge of the Son of God and become mature, attaining to the whole measure of the fullness of Christ. Then we will no longer be infants, tossed back and forth by the waves, and blown here and there by every wind of teaching and by the cunning and craftiness of men in their deceitful scheming. Instead, speaking the truth in love, we will in all things grow up into him who is the Head, that is, Christ. From him the whole body, joined and held together by every supporting ligament, grows and builds itself up in love, as each part does its work.*

There is a custom among certain Aboriginal tribes in Australia. At a predetermined time, each young person is entrusted with secret knowledge or a special skill vital to the tribe's survival. It may be directions to a watering hole or the medicinal benefits of a particular plant. No one else is given that information. In this way, each person becomes essential for the welfare of the whole community. Everyone has a role to play.

Paul explains that the whole Body of Christ will grow and flourish *"as each part does its work."* There are no insignificant body parts in the church (1 Corinthians 12:12-26). Each one is vital to the whole.

## Learning and Living Spiritual Gifts

There are four central passages in the New Testament that list spiritual gifts in the church. Because no list is exactly like the others, we conclude that these may not be the totality of spiritual gifts available to the church. Compare the gifts in Romans 12:6-8, 1 Corinthians 12:8-10, 1 Corinthians 12:28-30 and Ephesians 4:11 (see chart on next page).

| Spiritual Gifts in the Bible | | | |
|---|---|---|---|
| **Romans 12:6-8** | **1 Corinthians 12:8-10** | **1 Corinthians 12:28-30** | **Ephesians 4:11** |
| | Word of Wisdom | | |
| | Word of Knowledge | | |
| | Healing | Healing | |
| | Miracles | Miracles | |
| Prophecy | Prophecy | Prophecy | Prophecy |
| | Discerning of Spirits | | |
| | Tongues | Tongues | |
| | Interpretation of Tongues | Interpretation of Tongues | |
| | Faith | | |
| | | Apostles | Apostles |
| Teaching | | Teachers | Teaching |
| Serving | | Helps | |
| | | Administration | |
| Encouragement | | | |
| Giving | | | |
| Leadership | | | |
| Mercy | | | |
| | | | Evangelists |
| | | | Pastors |

Because spiritual gifts are so important to the building of Christ's church, it is important that each Christian know what gift(s) they have been given. A gift undiscovered goes unused.

The disciple can discover their own spiritual gifts through several means. First, they should search and study what the Bible teaches about spiritual gifts and their usefulness to the church. Second, they could take a "spiritual gifts inventory"—a diagnostic tool that helps a person understand their spiritual design. These tools are easily accessed online through a variety of sites and, while they are not determinative, they are a good place for a person to start in understanding their possible gifts. Third, the disciple may simply ask which gift(s) they think they may have or desire to have. Many people are more intuitive about their gifts than they may first think. Fourth, the disciple could consult with trusted, spiritual counselors—those who know the person well. Often, others can see in us what we cannot see in ourselves. Finally, they can look for success. People will often excel in what they're designed to do.

Although spiritual gifts bring great blessing to the church, there are coordinate dangers in the gifts at the same time. One danger is delegating corporate responsibility only to those with special ability. Sometimes, there is a need in the church that can be met by...anyone. No Christian should neglect encouraging others because they don't have the spiritual gift of encouragement. No one should resist serving or giving because they don't have the gifts of serving or generosity. Spiritual gifts equip Christians for greater service, but they do not release any Christians from basic ministry responsibility.

A second danger is veiwing spiritual gifts as a measure of maturity. Some spiritual gifts have greater public impact (preaching, teaching, prophecy, etc.). But, this in no way diminishes the importance of all other gifts. No Christian is elevated in status because they possess certain gifts (Romans 12:3). All believers are equally valuable in their ability and their humility.

With this second danger is a third one: using spiritual gifts apart from love. In the Corinthian church, the exercise of some gifts was causing greater disunity rather than unity. The reason, Paul revealed, was that those with the gift of tongues were not taking the rest of the church into consideration. Their gift had become an opportunity for their own self-promotion. This could happen with any spiritual gift. Pastors could preach without love for their flock. Leaders could lead out of their own self-importance. Those with the gift of administration could become controlling of others. Apart from love, spiritual gifts are nothing (1 Corinthians 13:1-3).

## A Word About the Gift of Tongues

Whenever the topic of spiritual gifts is discussed, questions about the "sign gifts" (tongues, miracles, word of knowledge) are raised, especially in regards to the gift of tongues. The modern Pentecostal view holds that the gift of tongues is the evidence of a special "baptism" of the Holy Spirit that takes place after the Christian's baptism into the Body of Christ and water baptism at conversion. This Holy Spirit blessing anoints the Christian for service and victorious living. The manifestation of this baptism is the phenomenon of tongues, which some conclude is an individual "prayer language"—

ecstatic, incomprehensible utterances—whereby the believer worships God.

There are two primary passages used to support this position: 1 Corinthians 13:1 and Romans 8:26.

*If I speak in the tongues of men and of angels, but have not love, I am only a resounding gong or a clanging cymbal.* (1 Corinthians 13:1)

*In the same way, the Spirit helps us in our weakness. We do not know what we ought to pray for, but the Spirit himself intercedes for us with groans that words cannot express.* (Romans 8:26)

These two passages speak about a "tongue of angels" and a "Holy Spirit groaning," both which seem to fit the Pentecostal view. However, closer inspection of these passages reveals the author's true intent. First, in 1 Corinthians 13:1, Paul never mentions the Holy Spirit. Second, he uses an if/then conditional statement which, in the original Greek, was a form of exaggeration. Paul did not actually claim that he or anyone else could speak in the language of angels. Third, the purpose of the passage was not to teach about languages or angels, but to teach about love.

We can only understand Romans 8:26 in the broader context of verses 18-27. Paul is considering the suffering that Christians undergo and mentions three "groans": the groaning of creation (v. 22), the groaning of the believer (v. 23) and the groaning of the Holy Spirit (v. 26). All three groans are in response to the bondage of creation, the suffering of sinful humanity and the great desire for all the world to be liberated at the coming of Jesus. Thus, the groaning of the Holy Spirit isn't a private prayer language, but the intercession of the Holy Spirit on the Christian's behalf.

So, what is the nature and purpose of tongues?

The first mention of tongues is in the book of Acts. Jesus told His disciples that they would *"receive power when the Holy Spirit comes on you; and you will be my witnesses in Jerusalem, and in all Judea and Samaria, and to the ends of the earth"* (Acts 1:8). Remember that Jesus' first followers were "unschooled, ordinary men" (Acts 4:13) and would need supernatural ability to accomplish the great mission of the Gospel ministry. When the disciples were gathered in the upper room, they were all filled with the Holy Spirit and *"began to speak in other tongues as the Spirit enabled them"* (Acts 2:4). The word "tongues" (plural) indicates that there were several tongues—not just one other—that were spoken.

As Peter began to preach his first sermon, notice what happened:

*Now there were staying in Jerusalem God-fearing Jews from every nation under heaven. When they heard this sound, a crowd came together in bewilderment, because each one heard them speaking in his own language. Utterly amazed, they asked: "Are not all these men who are speaking Galileans? Then how is it that each of us hears them in his own native language? Parthians, Medes and Elamites; residents of Mesopotamia, Judea and Cappadocia, Pontus and Asia, Phrygia and Pamphylia, Egypt and the parts of Libya near Cyrene; visitors from Rome (both Jews and converts to Judaism); Cretans and Arabs—we hear them declaring the wonders of God in our own tongues!" Amazed and perplexed, they asked one another, "What does this mean?"* (Acts 2:5-12)

Immediately after the first Christians received the Holy Spirit and spoke in "other tongues," the crowd in Jerusalem heard the strange sound and each foreign visitor heard the disciples "speaking in his own language." There is no question that the phenomenon of tongues was the God-given ability to disciples to enable otherwise uneducated men to have the ability to communicate the Gospel in previously unlearned languages. This gift was essential to the expansion of the Gospel reach around the world. The fruit of tongues was evident, not in greater spirituality of the disciples, but in the addition of 3000 new converts to the church in one day.

The manifestation of tongues appears two more times in the book of Acts. In Acts 10, Peter receives a vision of unclean animals and a command to "eat." This is a pivotal time in the expansion of the early church. After the vision, Peter is called to the house of Cornelius, a Gentile. He shares the truth of Jesus, and Cornelius' whole household believes. Luke describes the account, *"While Peter was still speaking these words, the Holy Spirit came on all who heard the message. The circumcised believers who had come with Peter were astonished that the gift of the*

*Holy Spirit had been poured out even on the Gentiles. For they heard them speaking in tongues and praising God."* (Acts 10:44-46)

The reason that Cornelius and his family began to speak in tongues was not for their sake, but for Peter's sake. Peter, a Jew, would not have expected that the Gospel was also for the "unclean Gentiles." But the outward manifestation of the Spirit convinced him that the Gospel was given to all because the Spirit had been poured out on the Gentiles just as He had been poured out on the Jewish Christians at Pentecost.

The next reference to tongues in Acts had the same purpose. In this instance, Paul was in Corinth (Acts 19), delivering the Gospel to Gentiles. Notice that Paul arrived to find "disciples" who had not yet received the Holy Spirit. They had been baptized with John's baptism, but were unclear regarding Jesus. In verse 4, Paul urged them to believe in the one coming after John—Jesus—and they were immediately baptized into Jesus' name. With this, they received the Holy Spirit and spoke in tongues.

This instance is not about believers receiving the Holy Spirit at a later time, but about disciples of John following John's teaching and having incomplete truth. Upon hearing the full Gospel, they placed their faith in Jesus and received the Holy Spirit at their conversion as all Christians do. The manifestation of tongues, like the earlier account, was to convince Paul, the most ardent Jew, that the Gospel was not for the Jew only.

With these two instances, it becomes clear that tongues were used to validate the authenticity of Gentile conversions. But, this wasn't the primary purpose of tongues. As in the first use of tongues at Pentecost, this spiritual gift was mainly used, not as a spiritual conversion marker, but as a church growth strategy. Early Christians were given the sudden ability to speak other known languages in order to reach beyond Jerusalem and Judea and into Samaria and even to the outer reaches of the earth. This helps us to understand the most extensive explanation of tongues in 1 Corinthians 14.

Before explaining this passage, it might be helpful to note that this is the only spiritual gift for which an entire chapter of Scripture is devoted. Paul's letter was intended to deal with the problem of disunity in the church, among other things. The widespread misunderstanding and misuse of tongues in the early church was creating division. The problem continues today. There is an unfortunate division between those who claim to speak in tongues and those whom they say "ought to."

If we use the consistent translation of "other known languages" as our understanding of tongues, we understand 1 Corinthians 14 in the following general sense: Paul makes a distinction between prophecy (preaching truth to the church) and speaking in tongues (communicating truth to foreign unbelievers). Paul's argument is that, when the church is gathered, prophecy is the most beneficial spiritual gift because it builds up the church. If a person with the gift of tongues (other known languages) speaks in the church without anyone interpreting, it has no benefit. The speaker edifies himself and God because he stewards the gift God gives, but he does not really help the church because no one understands. It would be no better than musical instruments that play random notes. This is why Paul states that *"in the church"* he would rather *"speak five intelligible words to instruct than ten thousand words in a tongue"* (v. 19). Tongues then, are *"for unbelievers"* (v. 22), not the church.

What, then, is the phenomenon that some Christians experience today that they describe as "speaking in tongues"? The answer is not easy. Most of these believers are genuine and God-seeking. With this in mind, all Christians must be charitable in our opinions of each other. Whatever we believe about this gift, let us do whatever is for the benefit of building up the church of Jesus Christ.

## SUMMARY

This chapter begins the final section in the spiritual pathway. The mission of God must become the mission of the church: the glory of God through the redemption of sinners. Those who BELONG to Christ and BECOME more like Him must go BEYOND to take Christ into their world so that God may be worshipped by all. This begins by going BEYOND into the church. Christians have been blessed to be a blessing to other believers by using their spiritual gifts in service to the church so that the church might be built up and have the most effective witness in the world. This chapter concluded with an explanation of the controversial gift of tongues.

## TAKE THE NEXT STEP

1. Before reading this chapter, how would you state the goal or mission of your church? How has this chapter changed your perspective?

2. Have you ever thought about God's mission for *your life*? How would you state it in your own words?

3. What instances in the Bible can you name where God's people had been "blessed to be a blessing"?

4. What are your spiritual gifts? How did you discover your gifts? If you don't know your spiritual gift(s), ask your pastor to direct you to an inventory that will help you discover them. In what way can you use your spiritual gift to serve your church?

5. What is your opinion regarding the spiritual gift of tongues? Do you believe the gift is operative today? If so, in what way?

6. What is the most important thing you learned from this chapter?

# BEYOND: INTO
# MY NEIGHBORHOOD

*Love the Lord your God...and love your neighbor as yourself.*
Jesus

On September 4, 2015, I received an email from a ministry friend in Budapest, Hungary. He wrote to share a sad report of Syrian migrants flooding his city—those who had recently fled their home country to find asylum throughout Europe. Minutes later, I stumbled upon news video of the refugee crisis. Some 4 million Syrians had been forced to flee for their lives. A very small fraction would qualify to be resettled somewhere around the world. It's the worst humanitarian crisis since World War II.

Our hearts broken, my wife, Tiffany, and I talked and agreed that we had been "blessed to be a blessing." We wanted to be part of a solution for any families arriving in the United States and our city. I contacted a friend who was the Executive Director of World Relief Fort Worth, a branch of one of only nine resettlement agencies in the country. He told me that a family of 8 Syrians was arriving in Texas the following week. We agreed to be their adoptive support family when they arrived at their new home..

| BELONG | | | BECOME | | BEYOND | | |
|---|---|---|---|---|---|---|---|
| TO CHRIST | TO COMMUNITY | TO CHURCH | INCIDENTAL TRANSFORMATION | INTENTIONAL TRANSFORMATION | INTO MY CHURCH | **INTO MY NEIGHBORHOOD** | INTO MY WORLD |

I posted about their upcoming arrival on social media and, instantly, dozens of people in our church jumped into action. Over the next six days, donors purchased new kitchen utensils, pots and pans, dishes and glasses, bed linens and pillows for eight, towels and washcloths, hygiene products, cleaning supplies, toys and books, a high chair, six child car seats, clothes, diapers, lamps, tables, beds and several weeks of groceries. The outpouring of generosity was overwhelming.

On September 11, the anniversary of the terrorist attacks on American soil, we met our travel-weary, Muslim family at the airport and helped them get settled in their new apartment. Over the next months, we helped our new friends get oriented to American culture. My wife accompanied the mother to the hospital for a check-up. We have helped them get their children enrolled in school. Each week since, I have been teaching the father English.

Because of the political animosity toward Muslims in America, several people—even Christians—have questioned the reasonableness of our efforts. Our response has been simple and biblical: "These are our neighbors." If we, as the church, miss caring for those in our own community, whether they have come by choice or by crisis, we have lost the mission of the church.

When Jesus charged His disciples to be His witnesses *"in Jerusalem, and in all Judea and Samaria, and to the ends of the earth"* (Acts 1:8), He was describing concentric circles of influence. Jerusalem was the capital city of Judaism, filled with devoted, God-sensitive people who would be easy for the Jewish disciples to connect with. Judea was the surrounding region, largely Jewish, and a natural area for ministry. Samaria was filled with nominal half-Jews who had compromised their religious convictions decades earlier. And "the ends of the earth" included a Gentile population. The disciples started their ministry in their own neighborhood first. Then they moved outward, in concentric circles of influence.

The missional church and missional disciples begin with their nearest neighbors, impacting people in their immediate community. When the teacher asked Jesus, "Who is my neighbor?" (Luke 10:29), Jesus replied with a parable and the lesson that a "neighbor" is anyone who is close enough for us to help.

## Christ and Culture

Unfortunately, too many churches do exactly the opposite of reaching their community. This isn't a recent problem. In 1951, Christian ethicist Richard Neibuhr wrote *Christ and Culture*, exploring the various ways that the church connects with the community around it. Among his five paradigms, two are relevant to this discussion. Some churches hold to a "Christ Against Culture" model, which puts the church in continual conflict with the pagan civilization around it. Adherents point to verses such as 1 Peter 1:15, *"But just as he who called you is holy, so be holy in all you do"* or 1 John 2:15, *"Do not love the world or anything in the world. If anyone loves the world, the love of the Father is not in him."* The Christian is to be set apart, uncontaminated by the evil in the world.

The result is that many churches view themselves as fortresses. Christians arrive on Sunday and are ushered into the retreat of biblical community. They enjoy "safe" music, "safe" teaching and "safe" relationships. The church barricades its doors, blocking out the contaminating and threatening influences of the world. The church fears the world or hates the world and, thus, positions itself *against* the world.

Evidence of this fortress mentality is subtle. Churches retreating from culture are so busy with activities that their members have no time to build relationships with their neighbors. These churches never open their facilities for community use. They rarely, if ever, provide resources to their community such as health clinics, disaster relief or food and clothing to the poor. Members may hear sermons instructing them to associate only with other Christians. Pastors preach with "insider language," assuming all those attending their worship services are people of faith. And, when needs arise, the community never imagines the church as the most likely source of help.

Neibuhr's paradigm of "Christ Transforming Culture" is opposite of the paradigm of "Christ Against Culture." In this model, the church views itself as a powerful change agent in the community. Rather than retreat from its community, Christians immerse themselves in their community to speak and show Gospel grace. This is the model we see in the early church:

*The apostles performed many signs and wonders among the people. And all the believers used to meet together in Solomon's Colonnade. No one else dared join them, even though they were highly regarded by the people. Nevertheless, more and more men and women believed in the Lord and were added to their number. As a result, people brought the sick into the streets and laid them on beds and mats so that at least Peter's shadow might fall on some of them as he passed by. Crowds gathered also from the towns around Jerusalem, bringing their sick and those tormented by impure spirits, and all of them were healed.* (Acts 5:12-16)

Notice that the early Christians operated under the power of the Holy Spirit, performing signs and wonders that validated their testimony. They did not manifest a cavalier spirituality so that unbelievers easily joined their ranks. Rather, the church grew through its ministry to its community. In fact, the church had such a positive reputation that unbelievers brought their sick and laid them in the streets with the hopes that Peter's shadow might pass over them and they be healed. The word "shadow" in this verse is the same word Luke uses in his Gospel when Mary is told that the Holy Spirit would "overshadow" her so that she would conceive the Christ (Luke 1:35) and when he writes about the clouds that overshadowed the disciples at Jesus' transfiguration (Luke 9:34). So, Peter's shadow wasn't some magical phenomenon. It was nothing less than the power of God working through Peter to heal the sick and set people free.

Don't miss this important principle: *The church is the shadow of God's presence and power in the world.* We don't possess original light. We are simply the reflection of Jesus who is the light of the world. As Jesus transforms the church, the church transforms the world. We are *"a chosen people, a royal priesthood, a holy nation, a people belonging to God, that you may declare the praises of him who called you out of darkness into his wonderful light"* (1 Peter 2:9).

## Turning On the Lights

So, how can Christians—the representation of the church—shine brightly in their community? Five words will help direct those who wish to go BEYOND into their neighborhoods: Love, Initiative, Grace, Hospitality and Sacrifice. We will explore each of these words in turn.

### Love

Love for people is fundamental to reaching people with the Gospel. When an expert in the law asked Jesus what the greatest commandments were, Jesus replied that all should love God and *"Love your neighbor as yourself"* (Mark 12:31). Love motivated the Father to send His Son (John 3:16), and love is what motivates the sons of God to take the good news of the Father to their neighbor.

Jesus illustrates several principles of love for our neighbor through His Parable of the Good Samaritan (Luke 10:30-37). First, love for our neighbor starts with seeing their broken humanity rather than how they might inconvenience us. Unlike the religious priest and Levite who passed by the injured traveler, the Samaritan realized the man's need and responded with loving compassion. The brokenness of the Samaritan's neighbor moved his heart to action.

Many years ago, I took my family to a fair near our city. As we walked from our parking place to the fair entrance, a man stopped me and begged for money. With my sons standing beside me, I asked the man his name, where he lived, and how long he had been homeless. After giving him a few dollars and walking away, my oldest son asked, "Dad, why did you ask him questions? And why did you keep looking into his eyes?"

I answered, "Son, I wanted to see him, not as a beggar, but as a human being." I wanted to understand his need. And, in seeing his need, I learned to love.

The second principle of love is this: Jesus' parable teaches that love is more than a feeling. Love shows itself in action. The Good Samaritan went to the injured traveler, bandaged his wounds and took him to a local town to recover. For him, love was more than a virtue. It was a verb. Just as God *"demonstrates His own love for us"* (Romans 5:8) and Jesus *"showed them the full extent of His love"* (John 13:1), so the church demonstrates and shows true love to the unlovely in its community. It's not enough for Christians to *say* they love others. They must take practical steps to show their love through words of encouragement, acts of service and generous provision.

This leads to a third principle of love: Love sacrifices its resources to bless others. The Samaritan gave his wine, bandages, donkey, money and time. True love gives. As mentioned in the last chapter, God blesses His people, not so they hoard the blessings for themselves, but so they extend the blessings of God to others. Churches should take inventory of "what they have" to discover how they might best bless their community. These resources include our home, financial savings, and the skills or abilities we have. Your home is where you show hospitality and welcome people into the world where Christ reigns. Demonstrate generosity by financially supporting your neighbor's band fundraiser, purchasing flowers for a funeral or providing meals for someone recovering from surgery. Offer what you own and the skills you have to repair a car, paint a room, help with taxes or provide a service. Whatever you have is what God can use to love your neighbors.

## Initiative

Reaching our neighbors requires initiative. The word means "the first in a series of actions" or "the setting in motion of something." It means that those inside the church make the first move in connecting with those outside the church. This movement sets in motion a Gospel relationship with others.

Many times, people came to Jesus. But Jesus didn't sit by, waiting for people to knock on His door. He took initiative. When he saw a crippled woman in the synagogue, Jesus called her forward and healed her (Luke 13:10). When He saw fishermen at the water's edge, He called them to be His disciples (Matthew 4:19). When he approached Jericho and noticed Zacchaeus perched in a tree, Jesus suggested they have dinner together (Luke 19:5). As He travelled through Samaria and stopped at a well, he asked a woman for a drink, starting a conversation that would lead to her life change (John 4:1-26). All of these acts of initiative can be traced back to the first act: Jesus taking the first step toward all of humanity in leaving His place in heaven to become a man.

In the relationship between God's people and their neighbors, Christians must "jump first." Don't expect your neighbors to invite themselves to your church. Don't think they will ask for help, though they may genuinely need it. Don't assume they know that you're ready, willing and able to help them repair a fence. Don't expect that the widow across the hall has family coming for Christmas. Don't be sure that they already know Jesus. Always take the first step.

And then, take a second step. After calling the first disciples, Jesus found them fishing again (Luke 5:1-11). This means that they had been invited into life with Jesus, but had reverted back to their former lifestyle. But Jesus didn't give up. He persisted in taking steps over and over again.

When I was in college, I served with Young Life, a ministry designed to reach high school students with the Gospel. One of the frequent and fundamental principles I learned was, "Never give up on a kid." After decades of ministry, Young Life had discovered that many teenagers initially oppose the Gospel. But, when leaders persist, taking second and third and fourth steps, some students are won over by unfailing love.

Christians are bound to face a hundred obstacles when it comes to reaching their neighbors. There will be a hundred opportunities to quit and retreat back to the fortress of our homes and church. But, we must never give up on our neighbors. Bill Bright, the founder of Campus Crusade for Christ, one of the most successful evangelistic ministries in the world, once said, "Success in witnessing is simply taking the initiative to share Christ in the power of the Holy Spirit, then leaving the results to God."

## Grace

Grace is undeserved blessing. It's not earned, but given freely, generously and unconditionally. We were saved, *"not because of anything we have done but because of his own purpose and grace"* (2 Timothy 1:9). We sing "Amazing Grace" because it confounds our human sensibilities that we would be loved without giving anything in return. This is how we are to love those around us.

We live in a world desperate for grace. Paul writes that all of creation groans under the weight of sin, longing for the full redemption of the children of God (Romans 8:18-27). Natural disasters, disease, corruption, abuse, violence, divorce, disappointment, hopelessness and fear abound in a graceless world. Next, compare your list with the list in this book. What changes might you make to either list? People everywhere are looking to fill the emptiness in their lives. The church of Jesus Christ has opportunity to give grace to those who need grace.

Showing grace requires the will to be gracious. In Luke 5, Jesus was approached by a man covered in leprosy (v. 12). The man fell before Jesus and begged Him, *"Lord, if you are willing, you can make me clean."* With that, Jesus reached out His hand and replied *"I am willing."* The issue at stake wasn't Jesus' *ability*, but His *availability*. In Mark's parallel account, we learn that Jesus was *"moved with compassion"* (Mark 1:41). He was willing to show grace because He could see the desperate needs in the world.

We reach our neighbors as we compassionately identify with their needs. No matter how successful, happy or carefree a person's life may seem, they are still plagued by the effects of sin until they meet Jesus Christ, the healer. We may not see it, but everyone is crying out for God to "have mercy" on them.

This grace is expressed in many ways. It starts with learning people's names. Get to know the last, the least and the lost—the marginalized people in your community. Throw a baby shower for the single mother. Offer to pay for the meal of a stranger in a restaurant. Help repair the homes of people who don't attend any church. Reach out to the widow and orphan. Organize your biblical community to clean up trash in your city. As with Tiffany and me befriending our Syrian friends, we hope the amazing grace of Jesus will lead them to know Him personally. But we serve them whether they do or don't.

## Hospitality

Above, we learned that true love moves toward people. Hospitality is the warmth and kindness that people experience when they come to us. Hospitality is a command for the people of God (Romans 12:13, 1 Peter 4:9, Titus 1:8) and is a qualification for church elders (1 Timothy 3:2). Christians are encouraged to show hospitality to strangers because some, without knowing it, have actually entertained angels (Hebrews 13:2).

Hospitality, whether in private homes or the house of God, the church, is a mixture of warmth, generosity and impartiality. It begins with genuine kindness toward people. It gives itself in gracious service, meeting the needs of guests. And it does so, not just for specific people, but for anyone who walks through the door.

I have a dear friend who lives 3 hours away and is the perfect example of hospitality. Whenever I need a personal retreat to get away and work or relax, he and his wife make their guest house overlooking a beautiful lake in Austin, Texas, available to me. Not only is the private apartment beautifully furnished and clean, but they insist on providing meals for me during my stay. During breaks, my friend, Jeff, takes me out in his boat on the water. And it's not just me. My friends are hospitable toward every guest who visits their home.

Every Christian and every church should be as welcoming. As you read this last sentence, ask yourself several questions: "Does every guest feel welcome in our church? Does anyone feel like an outsider? Is there a culture of kindness among my family? Would anyone ever discern a prejudicial or judgmental spirit in me? Am I a servant?" Unless there is hospitality, we will be ineffective in reaching our neighbors.

## Sacrifice

Financial investors know that, without a risk of assets, they will likely not enjoy a good return. In physical fitness, trainers claim, "No pain, no gain." Fruit requires planting, watering, cultivation…the hard work of farming. Similarly, if missional disciples wish to truly impact their community, they must be willing to give themselves away, to sacrifice.

This is the essence of the Gospel. Jesus was born a man and allowed His glorious splendor to be obscured. He gave up His divine prerogatives and laid down His life for people. He sacrificed His blood for sinners. He gave, we received—mission accomplished.

When I was in college, one of my friends lost all of his possessions in an apartment fire. Many people came to his aid to donate items, but one donation I will never forget. The student was needing clothes for an upcoming business interview and a mutual friend offered him several dress shirts, slacks and shoes. As he handed off the assortment of clothes, the donor pulled one hanging shirt out of the batch and said, "If you don't mind, when you're finished, I'd like that shirt back."

At first, I was taken back by the request and even concluded that his contribution was less than sacrificial if he "wanted something back." Then it occurred to me, he was offering his best. While other people might have given things that were left over and the extra from their life that they would never miss, this man was giving what was meaningful. He was expressing true sacrifice.

In 2 Samuel 24:24, David decides, *"I will not offer to the Lord my God that which costs me nothing."* If our mission is the way that we worship God, then we offer to God—and our neighbors—our very best. Sacrifice is essential for mission. A Christian cannot effectively impact their community without their mission costing something.

## Stepping Into Your Neighborhood

Several years ago, a new school was constructed two miles away from Pantego Bible Church. When the doors of John T. White Elementary opened, the classrooms were filled with mostly lower-income, underperforming children from single-parent homes. This means that the children would be difficult to teach and discipline, parents would be largely uninvolved in their child's education, and pressure would be significant for teachers. However, our church considered this a great opportunity in our neighborhood.

A group of staff leaders met with the principal of the school and offered our resources. A group of people, including staff and lay leaders, began to tutor first graders in reading. We began an after-school program that shared the gospel weekly with the 100 children who attended. Our church children's ministry wrote a series of "character development" classes to teach at the school. Our women's ministry honors the teachers and administrators several times a year by hosting a breakfast or luncheon for them, giving them small gifts and helping them set up their classrooms. Our church provides school supplies for teachers and students each year. The school holds its fifth grade "graduation" in our church worship center every May. And, whenever the school needs extra volunteers to help judge a science fair, or help at a special field day or help set up an auditorium for a parents' program, they call Pantego Bible Church. On one trip to the school to meet my first grade friend for a tutoring session, his teacher introduced me to her students, "Class, this is the pastor of the church down the street...the church that loves us." Mission accomplished!

There are many ways for each church and individual Christians to move into their neighborhood and have similar success. The following are general suggestions to help you think about your and your church's local mission.

**Serve Schools.** Just like Pantego Bible Church blessed John T. White Elementary (and four other schools in our city), find ways to help the schools in your neighborhood. When you serve schools, you serve an emerging generation. Schools are often under-funded and under-resourced. Tutor children. Bless teachers. Provide supplies. Send workers to clean, construct and repair. After sharing this vision at a conference in Burundi, one young leader named Hypolite caught a vision to begin serving in his son's school. Months later, he sent me an excited email explaining that he had given several wall calendars to the school to help teachers schedule their lessons. A small act communicated great love.

**Help the Homeless.** Jesus said that the poor will always be among us (Matthew 26:11). This is the announcement of great need. The church's greatest demonstration of grace is to those who have no possibility of returning the favor. Find the homeless in your community and serve them. Feed them. Clothe them. Provide haircuts and medical care. Offer a place for them to stay during extreme weather. Support ministries in your area that do the same.

**Protect the Widow and Orphan.** True religion, James explains, is to *"look after orphans and widows in their distress"* (James 1:27). These are the most vulnerable of our society and need special attention. Just as Jesus came to adopt us as children of God and become a husband to His bride, the church, so the people of God must become fathers and husbands to those in their community. Advocate for the orphan and support foster families. Give preference to single mothers. Protect women fleeing domestic violence. Help meet the physical and relational needs of the widow in your community.

**Bless Public Servants.** The Bible commands Christians to honor those who serve them (1 Thessalonians 5:12). This verse, of course, means to show proper respect to spiritual leaders. But the general principle may be applied to other public servants. Honor those who serve in public positions in your community: police, firemen, judges and local officials. Esteem them among your congregation and let them know that your church wishes to cooperate with their good community policies.

**Give a Second Chance.** Everyone makes mistakes. This means everyone needs a second chance. This is especially true of those who have served time in jail for their mistakes or who have worked through a recovery process for their destructive addictions. The church serves its community, not by pronouncing judgment against sinners, but by offering hope. Visit those in prison. Welcome ex-offenders into your fellowship. Support ministries, such as Celebrate Recovery, that offer a step-by-step pathway to freedom.

**Visit the Sick.** The church has the greatest opportunity for gracious ministry among those who are sick or dying. Visit those who have been hospitalized or bedridden at home. Pray for them. Read to them. Just be with them. One African pastor explained that, in his region, families of those who were sick were required to provide meals to patients. False religions were gaining ground because they would visit the sick and bring meals that families could not afford. This act of kindness was winning people to other faiths. What a powerful testimony of grace when the church cares, not only for its own, but for outsiders as well.

**Celebrate Weddings/Attend Funerals.** We connect with our community when we "rejoice with those who rejoice and weep with those who weep" (Romans 12:15). These life-change milestones are significant for our neighbors. When we step into their world by bringing a gift or a meal, we show the love of Jesus who made room in His schedule to attend a wedding and grieve with others at a funeral. Take an additional step by remembering the one-year anniversary of these life events.

**Support Other Churches.** All Christian churches worship the same

God and should have the same goal. One way to demonstrate your Kingdom commitment is to support other churches in your neighborhood. These churches don't have to be of the same denomination or theological conviction. Affirm their importance in your city. Encourage their ministry. Help them succeed. They will appreciate it and your community will take notice of this unity.

On my second trip to Africa, I was teaching pastors about the importance of going BEYOND into their local community. One young leader shared over lunch the most beautiful story of this principle. As he and several other Christians wondered how they might make a difference in their neighborhood, they realized that many of the children were dirty and didn't have the luxury of indoor plumbing to wash each day. So, their little church went into their neighborhood and set up "stations" where they could give children a bath. Along the way, the servants told the children the truth of God's great love for them.

When the children returned home clean, their parents asked, "What happened to you? Why do you look so different?"

The children replied, "God washed us."

This is the church in action in their neighborhood. In practical ways, we serve our communities and share the love of a God who "washes" each one of us. If God determines the times and seasons and exact places where people will live (Acts 17:26), He has placed your neighbors where they live and He has placed you where you are in your community. You are not where you are by accident. You are there to witness to the greatness of God and to help those who are far from God "reach out and find Him" (v. 27). Discover how you can go BEYOND, into your neighborhood, for the glory of God.

## SUMMARY

This chapter continues the final step in the spiritual pathway by encouraging the church and those inside each church to go BEYOND into their local community. Our missional impact requires love, initiative, grace, hospitality and sacrifice. As we consider God's providence in placing us and our churches in specific places, we should explore specific ways to minister in our communities.

# TAKE THE NEXT STEP

1. Generally speaking, does Jesus' church have a good or poor reputation in your city? Why? If you are a Christian, what is your posture toward your community: For it or against it?

2. How would you describe Christians and churches who have adopted the paradigm of "Christ Transforming Culture"?

3. How would you rate your life in regards to love, initiative, grace, hospitality and sacrifice? Which of these virtues need work?

4. Believing God has providentially placed you in the neighborhood, community, school or job where you are, what opportunities are available for you to better minister to those nearest to you?

5. What is the most important thing you learned from this chapter?

# BEYOND: INTO MY WORLD

*...All peoples on earth will be blessed through you.*
Genesis 12:3

God's heart is for people...all people.

God so loved the *world* that He sent His Son, Jesus, to save the world. His plan, from the beginning, was not to bless a specific group of people only, but for His blessings *to* them to flow *through* them to the nations. When the Lord made His covenant promise to Abram, the benefits were not only for his descendants, but so that "all peoples on earth" would be blessed through them (Genesis 12:3).

This global mission theme is threaded throughout Scripture. God said that He would unleash his power against Pharaoh, so that His *"name might be proclaimed in all the earth"* (Exodus 9:16). His people Israel were to be a "kingdom of priests" (Exodus 19:6)—mediators to bring the godless everywhere to God. After crossing the Jordan, God's people set up a memorial *"so that all the peoples of the earth might know that the hand of the LORD is powerful"* (Joshua 4:24) and, while living in their land, they were to welcome the alien and stranger (Deuteronomy 10:19).

| BELONG | | | BECOME | | BEYOND | | |
|---|---|---|---|---|---|---|---|
| TO CHRIST | TO COMMUNITY | TO CHURCH | INCIDENTAL TRANSFORMATION | INTENTIONAL TRANSFORMATION | INTO MY CHURCH | INTO MY NEIGHBORHOOD | INTO MY WORLD |

When the ark of God was brought into Jerusalem, David prayed,

*Sing to the LORD, all the earth;*
*proclaim his salvation day after day.*
*Declare his glory among the nations,*
*his marvelous deeds among all peoples.* (1 Chronicles 16:23-24)

Similarly, Solomon prayed at the temple dedication *"that all the peoples of the earth may know your name and fear you"* (1 Kings 8:43). The psalmist declares, *"proclaim among the nations what he has done"* (Psalm 9:11) and, *"I will praise you among the nations, O LORD"* (Psalm 18:49) and,

*The desert tribes will bow before him*
*and his enemies will lick the dust.*
*The kings of Tarshish and of distant shores*
*will bring tribute to him;*
*the kings of Sheba and Seba*
*will present him gifts.*
*All kings will bow down to him*
*and all nations will serve him.* (Psalm 72:9-11)

The prophets looked forward to the ultimate Kingdom rule of God. Through Isaiah, the Lord announced that He would make Himself known among the Gentiles:

*I will set a sign among them, and I will send some of those who survive to the nations—to Tarshish, to the Libyans and Lydians (famous as archers), to Tubal and Greece, and to the distant islands that have not heard of my fame or seen my glory. They will proclaim my glory among the nations.* (Isaiah 66:9)

And through Malachi, He spoke His eternal purpose:

*My name will be great among the nations, from the rising to the setting of the sun. In every place incense and pure offerings will be brought to my name, because my name will be great among the nations," says the LORD Almighty.* (Malachi 1:11)

When Jesus was born, angels announced the good news that would be *"for all the people"* (Luke 2:10), and when Jesus was presented in the temple, Simeon rejoiced, *"For my eyes have seen your salvation, which you have prepared in the sight of all people"* (Luke 2:30-31).

Jesus commanded believers to *"go and make disciples of all nations"* (Matthew 28:19) and to the early church, He charged that they would be His witnesses *"in Jerusalem, and in all Judea and Samaria, and to the ends of the earth"* (Acts 1:8). Paul declared that the Gospel was *"first to the Jew, then to the Gentile"* (Romans 1:16) and then came full circle to the Abrahamic Covenant when he wrote, *"The Scripture foresaw that God would justify the Gentiles by faith, and announced the gospel in advance to Abraham: 'All nations will be blessed through you'"* (Galatians 3:8). Finally, John envisioned a multitude *"from every nation, tribe, people and language, standing before the throne and in front of the Lamb"* (Revelation 7:9).

Remarkably, these are but a handful among many Scriptures that affirm that God's goal has always been to reveal His glory among *all* people. This has been His mission throughout all of history. And, this is the mission God has given His church.

## Unreached But Not Unreachable

Unfortunately, though this is God's Great Commission, there are still many people who have yet to hear the Gospel of Jesus. The "nations" or "peoples" in the Bible refer to the unique people groups scattered across the world. At Babel, languages were confused because of the sinful pride of people (Genesis 11:1-9), and since then, about 13,000 unique ethno-linguistic groups have emerged. In the last 2000 years, approximately 70% of those groups have been "reached" with the Gospel. That is, at least 2% of their population is Christian—a viable witness able to evangelize their own people.

This means that 30% of the world's population—4000 people groups or about 3 billion people—is "unreached." They have never heard the Gospel of Jesus and there are no missionaries or churches among them. The great majority of these unreached people (95%) live in the 10/40 Window, the region between 10° and 40° north of the equator. This includes much of China, India, the Middle East and

North Africa—people such as the 357,000 Kanuri/Yerwa people in South Sudan, the 132,000 Darzada people in Pakistan, the 3800 Madasi Kuruva people in India and the 200 Samre people in Cambodia.

Imagine so many people, not people who have rejected Jesus, but who have not even heard His name! These people represent the church's present mission in the world. In Romans 10:14-15, Paul asks, *"How, then, can they call on the one they have not believed in? And how can they believe in the one of whom they have not heard? And how can they hear without someone preaching to them? And how can they preach unless they are sent?"* For all the nations to hear, the church must go to them.

However, though the need is urgent, many churches continue to focus much of their mission on those who have *already* been reached with the Gospel. For example, in the United States, 95 cents of every dollar collected for ministry stays in the country. Four and one-half cents is directed to missionary efforts around the world, but this money is directed to those who have already been reached. Only one-half of one cent is directed to reaching unreached people.

Among all churches in the world, only 10% of missionary efforts are directed to unreached people. Of the 430,000 missionaries around the world, only 2-3% of them are ministering among unreached people, and 40% of the global church's work is taking place within 10 of the most oversaturated countries on the planet. In 100 AD, there were 12 unreached people groups for each young congregation. But, today, there are 1,000 congregations worldwide for each unreached group. It is quite possible to go BEYOND and finish the task.

## Reaching the World Beyond

Every church, no matter what its economic resource, geographic region or denominational affiliation, has a gospel mandate to go BEYOND into the world. And, if a church is committed to fulfilling the Great Commission, God will surely honor its desire by making its obedience possible. I've seen this firsthand.

In 2012, I traveled with several pastors to Cuba in order to train church leaders. In one location, an American Missions Pastor preached a sermon urging those present to make missions the goal of their churches. Given the political and economic limitations of the Cuban church, we expected their missionary work to be relatively small. However, at the end of the sermon, the group introduced a missionary couple who had been raising support to go to South America and was ready to depart. We saw firsthand that no church is too poor or too restricted to go into the world.

But, where should God's people focus their efforts? What is the most strategic mission?

Generally speaking, global mission must include two prongs: proclamation and demonstration. In His ministry, Jesus did both. His Gospel came with both word and deed. He preached the Good News and then proved the Gospel with good works. These equal and complimentary sides of mission look like this:

| Proclamation | Demonstration |
|---|---|
| Revelation | Compassion |
| Good News | Good Works |
| Preach | Serve |
| Speak | Act |
| Tell | Show |
| Pronounce | Prove |

Gospel proclamation means that we unapologetically promote the truth of Jesus Christ as Messiah to the world. We must counter false gospels and preach the true Gospel (see chapter 2) by extending the Word of God into every region of the world. Such ministries include Bible translation, evangelistic crusades, door-to-door evangelism, showing the Jesus Film, or using an event to attract an audience who will be open to hearing about Jesus. One missionary friend invites American Christians to perform western dances in the city squares of Spain. These "festivals" are significant family events that include personal testimonies and a clear Gospel presentation as their central feature. Hundreds of people in Spain have begun personal relationships with Jesus Christ as result.

Several years ago, I was invited to teach a parenting conference offered to people who had enrolled their children in a private school in China. The school was operated by a Christian mission, but families were not required to be Christians for their children to attend. The parenting conference was biblically-oriented and the Gospel was clearly presented. In this way, helping mothers and fathers was secondary to the greater goal of proclaiming Jesus.

Every year, a small group from our church travels to another region of the United States to share the Gospel of Jesus with Mormons who have arrived to celebrate an annual festival. The great majority of attendees are thoroughly entrenched in Mormonism, which doesn't teach the true Gospel of Jesus and salvation by grace alone. Our missionaries weave in and out of the crowds, starting conversations with strangers, hoping to engage attendees with the truth and proclaim Jesus as the only way to God.

There is no substitute for speaking the truth of Jesus where He has not been announced (Romans 1:16, 15:20). In every missionary effort, the church must announce the problem of sin and death and the salvation of Jesus Christ by grace through faith. People cannot be saved unless they *hear* the Gospel proclaimed.

Gospel demonstration prepares the way for and validates Gospel proclamation. Jesus told His people to *"let your light shine before men, that they may see your good deeds and praise your Father in heaven"* (Matthew 5:16). Likewise, Peter commanded, *"Live such good lives among the pagans that, though they accuse you of doing wrong, they may see your good deeds and glorify God on the day he visits us"* (1 Peter 2:12). Whereas hypocrisy—an inconsistency between personal profession and practice—is one of the greatest deterrents to the Gospel, the church that lives what it believes can be one of the most compelling witnesses.

To demonstrate the Gospel is to live the character of the Gospel: showing grace, forgiveness, sacrifice, service, humility, love, compassion, generosity and blessing to others. It means that Christians live out the blessings of God to others (see Genesis 12:3, Psalm 67:1-2). Paul describes this "overflow" of blessing in 2 Corinthians 1:3-5:

*Praise be to the God and Father of our Lord Jesus Christ, the Father of compassion and the God of all comfort, who comforts us in all our troubles, so that we can comfort those in any trouble with the com-*

*fort we ourselves have received from God. For just as the sufferings of Christ flow over into our lives, so also through Christ our comfort overflows.*

Gospel demonstration may express itself in many ways: caring for orphans or widows, repairing homes, providing disaster relief, offering a medical clinic among the poor, constructing a water well, or helping college students learn English, just to name a few. Each initiative meets a specific human need in order to prepare hearts for Jesus. As one missionary explained, "No one hears the Gospel on an empty stomach."

In his 1997 book, *The Rise of Christianity: How the Obscure, Marginal Jesus Movement Became the Dominant Religious Force in the Western World in a Few Centuries*, Rodney Stark observes that the early church gained a credible hearing because of the compassionate way it demonstrated the ethic of the Gospel by meeting physical needs. He notes,

[The] rise to dominance of Christianity in the Roman Empire was greatly facilitated by the smallpox and measles epidemics which hit the Empire in 165 and 251 and killed between ¼ and $1/3$ of the population. While the just and the unjust alike died, the pagan religions, in the persons of their priests, fled the scene, concerned only for self-preservation. The philosophers, too, sat around musing abstractly about the decline of Virtue in an elderly world. People shunned sick relatives and friends, leaving them to die alone and unmourned. Meanwhile, the Christians invested themselves in caring for the sick and dying–even at the cost of themselves getting sick and dying. As well, Christianity provided, via the doctrine of the resurrection of the dead and the hope of living with Christ forever, a far better foundation for seeing life as meaningful even amidst the horror of the epidemics. While the pagans reacted in sheer terror or prattling acceptance, the Christians lived a life amidst death that powerfully illustrated the superiority of their Faith. Christian nursing of the sick, in turn, greatly aided survival rates during the plagues. The pagans saw a difference in the religions, and many of them wanted what the Christian Faith had to offer. Such a testimony is a significant reason why Christianity triumphed in the ancient world. Its culture was simply superior to that of the pagans.

In the context of this crisis, it was as important for the church to *show* the Gospel as to *speak* it.

In 2010, I served with a team of dentists who traveled to Ethiopia to offer their professional services to people in several regions. Over the course of a week, they cleaned teeth, filled cavities and performed extractions on hundreds of people. As patients waited for care, our team shared the story of how God meets all of our needs through His Son, Jesus.

Another team returned to that country and began a partnership with an orphan care ministry to support the work of a church in one region. The team also worked with that church to offer a free health clinic to people in the community. And, learning about the need for a water well in a nearby town, they agreed to adopt this project as a tangible way to meet human need.

Gospel proclamation and Gospel demonstration go hand in hand. To share good news without good works may lack compassion. To do good works without verbally sharing the Good News falls short of the purpose of mission, meeting people's temporal, physical needs without addressing their eternal, spiritual needs. The missional disciple must always remember that *"faith comes by hearing"* (Romans 10:17).

## 5 Good Strategies

Once a Christian makes a personal commitment to global missions, they will quickly discover thousands of opportunities to engage. In fact, the deluge of mission organizations and initiatives can be overwhelming for the disciple who simply wants to go BEYOND in the world. Recently, at Pantego Bible Church, we began to narrow our focus and direct our global missions sending and spending to five very strategic areas of greatest need:

## Disciplemaking Among the Most Unreached

As noted above, 30% of the world still hasn't heard the Gospel of Jesus. Rather than investing only in initiatives among the already-reached people, we have chosen to focus more and more of our attention on the least reached people of the world. To be sure, these areas may be more difficult and, because of security reasons, will likely require partnerships with specialized organizations. But, the investment is worth it.

## Bible Translation Among the Bible-less

Among the 7000 languages spoken in the world today, fewer than 600 have a complete translation of the Old and New Testaments. One billion people have no part of the Bible translated into their language! While Bible translation used to take decades for each language, new tools have accelerated the process, making it possible for more people to have God's Word in their mother tongue. In a few cases, churches may have gifted personnel who can help the Bible translation process. But, in most cases, a church participates in this strategy by financially adopting part or all of a project. Bible translation ministries expect that, by 2025, the last translation of the New Testament may begin!

## Leadership Training

Leadership training is an integral part of reaching the unreached and getting the Bible into their languages. Fewer than 10% of pastors around the world have access to ministry training, and 85% of churches around the world are led by leaders with no formal theological training. A church that wishes to impact the world must begin by impacting leaders. Invest in training ministries and theological resources for pastors everywhere.

## Global Justice

God's people are called to "do justice" (Micah 6:8, Isaiah 61:8) because God always does what is just and right. Justice means caring for the needs of the vulnerable in such a way that their rights are protected and their lives are afforded dignity as those created in the image of God. This means alleviating modern day slavery and sex trafficking, providing food and clothing to the most impoverished and serving the refugee.

## Multiplying Healthy Churches

The Gospel is extended as new churches are planted. Missional churches don't only plant multiple "branches" of themselves in their own region. They desire to see healthy churches planted even in the most remote and unchurched regions of the world. This Kingdom mindset wishes to see *the* church grow, not just *my* church grow.

## Stepping Out

It is a significant step for any follower of Jesus to move beyond themselves, into their local community and, eventually, into the world. This transition will not happen naturally or immediately for any church. There are several intentional steps that will help the missional disciple go global.

**Affirm the biblical mandate.** Search and discover God's redemptive plan starting in Genesis 3 and moving to the Abrahamic Covenant (Genesis 12:1-5; see p. 126). Notice how the Jews were "blessed to be a blessing" and how God has always had the nations in mind regarding His Kingdom. Emphasize the five "commissions" in Matthew 28:18-20, Mark 16:15-16, Luke 24:47, John 20:21 and Acts 1:8. Remember that the Gospel is for the Jew and Gentile everywhere (Romans 1:16).

**Make a personal commitment.** For many years, Pantego Bible Church had very little missional impact, and I was hired to reignite our missional fervor. Within 6 months of arriving, I and several lay leaders from our church travelled to China on a vision trip to explore mission opportunities for our church. I wanted our church to not only hear me *speak* about missions, but to see me *model* a mission commitment. If we want our spouse, our children and our Christian friends to catch a missional vision with us, we will have to model the mission first. You may start this journey alone before anyone joins you.

**Start local.** In the last chapter, we considered how we make an impact in our neighborhood and community. If we don't serve locally, we will not likely expand our influence globally. Local ministry enables Christians to express their gifts and passions in an environment that is familiar and requires fewer resources. Often, as people are inspired by the effectiveness of their ministry in their community, they are more open to opportunities to serve further beyond.

Another benefit of local ministry is that, sometimes, God brings the nations to our doorstep. In larger urban areas, international students will study at universities or businesses will welcome foreign partners. Or refugees may be resettled in your city. What better way to be a blessing to the nations without leaving your country.

**Pray for workers.** Jesus said, *"The harvest is plentiful but the workers are few. Ask the Lord of the harvest, therefore, to send out workers into his harvest field"* (Matthew 9:37-38). The emphasis is on the multiplication of workers for a ready harvest and the dependence on God to raise up laborers. But, in the very discipline of praying for these things, God sensitizes a congregation to this need and the Christian's responsibility. There is no question that prayer moves God. But, when asked, "Does prayer change God?" a pastor responded, "Prayer changes *me*!" As disciples pray for the harvest fields and new workers, God may use prayers to impact those who are praying, cultivating a greater global perspective.

**Make mission a financial commitment.** You can start making an impact on the nations with your bank account. In addition to your faithful tithe to your church, identify missionaries and missions that are near to your heart. Jesus said that our money will follow our heart. At the same time, our heart will increasingly follow our financial commitment.

## A Word About Going

Global missions requires great resource and much energy. So, it's not surprising that some people will push back with excuses. The most common excuse I hear is, "Why would we focus on ministry in another country when there are so many needs in our city right here?"

There is, of course, some truth to this perception: There *are* many needs in our cities and our country. And, the Christian who cultivates a global vision shouldn't neglect the ministry opportunities around them. Just because there is poverty in my community doesn't mean I shouldn't help people impacted by floods or tornadoes in another state. And, just because there are many people who don't know Jesus here doesn't give me reason not to take Jesus to others "over there." There are any number of compelling reasons why the disciple of Jesus should have a global focus.

First, Jesus commanded it. In Matthew 28:18-20, Jesus charged His people to "make disciples of all nations." To reach our neighbors only is to neglect the clear command of Jesus and the mission of God that all the nations of the earth will be blessed.

Second, we have more resources. If you live in the United States, you may already know that we consume a disproportionate amount of the world's resources. We have more pastors, seminary professors, books, programs and curriculums that other countries, especially those in the developing world. It is good and generous stewardship for God's people to share their material, intellectual and personal wealth with the rest of the world.

Third, the need around the world is much greater than the need here. In the United States, especially, opportunities abound for people to encounter Christian influences and attend a church. Of course, this doesn't mean that people are "more" Christian or that Christianity has the same influence that it once had. But, compared to many regions of the world which have become secularized or have little or no Christian witness, the United States is thoroughly saturated with ministry.

Finally, God uses experiences BEYOND to stretch us beyond our ordinary capacity. Global mission pushes the envelope of faith. And, those who venture into uncharted places get to witness God at work in extraordinary ways and grow in their relationship with Him.

## SUMMARY

In this chapter, the Christian is challenged to go BEYOND, into the world. Having confirmed that the Gospel is for every nation, tribe and tongue, and realizing there are still many unreached people around the world, the mission mandate is urgent. Therefore, each disciple must have a commitment to Gospel proclamation and Gospel demonstration. Five important areas of focus include making disciples among the most unreached, translating the Bible for the Bibleless, training leaders, practicing global justice and multiplying healthy churches everywhere.

## TAKE THE NEXT STEP

1. Why might some Christians/churches miss that the Gospel is intended for *all* people? Why do some neglect global missions?

2. How do you feel knowing that there are so many unreached people in the world? What will you do with this information?

3. Do you tend to default to Gospel proclamation or demonstration? Why? Why do you think it is important to have both?

4. Which of the five missional strategies is most exciting to you? How might you or your church begin to participate in one or more of these strategies?

5. As you look at the steps toward becoming a missional disciple, which of them can you begin to implement immediately?

6. What is the most important thing you learned from this chapter?

# GETTING THERE FROM HERE

*Show me your ways, O LORD, teach me your paths.*
Psalm 25:4

This book has been about a spiritual progress. It was written to help followers of Jesus move along the spiritual pathway to greater missional discipleship. Hopefully, the chapters have aroused in you a holy discontent—a desire to take *new* steps and *more* steps in your spiritual life. The question you may now be asking is, "How do I get to there from here? How do I make spiritual progress?" This final chapter will help you take the next steps in your life with Jesus.

## Where Are You?

To get from here to there, you must know where "here" is. A map is useful in helping me reach my destination, but only if I know my present location. In the same way, every disciple must first understand where they presently stand on the spiritual pathway before they can move forward. Now is a good time to ask yourself the question, "Where am I?" Make a self-assessment based on the steps of the spiritual pathway described throughout this book:

**Do I BELONG to Jesus Christ?** Have I placed my faith in Him for my salvation and am I confident of His death alone for the forgiveness of my sins? Have I been baptized in obedience to Jesus as an outward testimony of my changed life? Do I know my spiritual story?

**Do I BELONG to biblical community?** Do I meet regularly with other Christian friends who care for me and challenge me to live more like Jesus? Is our meeting together more substantive than just a "dinner club?" Are we "doing life together," growing deeper with one another and going deeper in a relationship with God?

**Do I BELONG to my church?** Am I a casual consumer or a committed member, as reflected in my unity, ministry, generosity, and submission to authority? Is church simply what I do when there's nothing else to do, or do I make my weekly connection with the people of God a high priority?

**Am I incidentally BECOMING more like Jesus Christ?** Do I discern that the Holy Spirit of God has been transforming my character, my convictions, my confidence, my contentment, my biblical comprehension and my compassion for ohers? Am I experiencing freedom from the bondage of sin to any degree? Am I any different than I was two or ten years ago?

**Am I intentionally BECOMING more like Jesus Christ?** Do I cooperate with God for my life change? Do I take responsibility in my sanctification by personally reading God's Word, studying the Bible with others, reading good books about the spiritual life, connecting in accountable relationships, memorizing scripture, getting counseling, or attending retreats, conferences or seminars that would greatly help me? Am I maturing in vision, knowledge, character and skills?

**How am I going BEYOND into my church?** Do I use my spiritual gifts for the benefit of the body of Christ by serving in ministry? Do I give more than I receive at my church? Am I personally committed to helping my church fulfill God's mission in the world?

**How am I going to BEYOND into my neighborhood?** Do I consider my home, my school or my workplace as strategic mission fields for me to make God known to others around me? Have I shared the Gospel of Jesus Christ with anyone recently? Do I have compassion for the lost, the least and the last who live around me? Do I reflect the light of Jesus Christ to those who do not know Him?

**How am I going BEYOND into my world?** Do I have a great desire for all people in all places to know Jesus? What global mission or missionaries do I support with my prayers and financial resources? Have I made Bible translation, leadership development, disciple-making among the reached, church multiplication or global justice possible around the world? Do I believe that Jesus is for all the nations?

This personal inventory isn't intended to shame anyone. Every Christ-follower can always find areas of needed growth. But, by asking questions like the ones above, the Christian is better able to discern where they are presently. If, at any point, you have more "no" responses than "yes" responses, this is where you "are." For example, the person who answers "yes" to the first set of questions (Belonging to Christ) and "yes" to the second group of questions (Belonging to community), but "no" to many of the questions in the third group discovers they have not really learned what it means to "belong to church." In other words, they are a Christian who enjoys biblical community, but they have not yet learned the importance of having a true commitment to Christ's church. This is where they are. And they will have difficulty moving further along the spiritual pathway until they address this step.

As another example, consider the individual who answers "yes" to most or all of the questions in sections 1-4; however, the questions in section 5 (Intentionally becoming more like Jesus Christ) do not reflect their current situation. We could conclude that this person is connected to Jesus, biblical community and church and, while they are experiencing some degree of transformation, they have not yet learned the importance of taking responsibility for their spiritual growth. They are a Christian fed by others, but they have not learned to feed themselves. This is where they are.

## Take the Next Step

Knowing where you are, it's now time to take the next step. What follows are very practical suggestions to help you move from your present place to the next place along the spiritual pathway.

**Stepping onto the Path:** If you do not yet belong to Jesus Christ, this is the first and most important step you can take. If you are persuaded by the problem of your sin and believe that Jesus Christ is your Savior, sent from God, then it is imperative that you trust Him with your life. It is time for you to place your faith in Jesus, surrender your life to Him, and become a child of God. Review pages 29-31 and then pray. Confess your sins to God and declare that Jesus alone is your salvation. Tell a Christian friend about this life-changing decision. And make plans to be baptized as soon as possible. You have begun the spiritual journey.

**From Christ to Community:** If you are a Christian but have not yet connected in biblical community, it's time to take this step. Many churches have "on ramps" for attendees to join a community within their church (sometimes referred to as home groups, small groups, missional communities, etc.). Ask your pastor how to join one of these groups or ask a friend who attends a group if you may join theirs. Your church doesn't have to have an organized program for you to gather a few Christian friends together and begin meeting. Remember, successful biblical community is built around *proximity* (people living close enough to one another to easily connect), *frequency* (people connecting with one another on a regular basis), and *availability* (people who truly want to be with each other ).

**From Community to Church:** Remember that there is a big difference between attending church and belonging to a church. It's time for you to move from being a consumer to a committed member. Attend the membership class of your church. Support the Gospel ministry of your church by giving regularly and generously. Don't just attend the worship service, but connect with classes and special events held by your church. One unmistakable proof that a person belongs to church is that they invite their neighbors to join them.

**From Connection to Transformation:** If you BELONG to Christ, community and church, you *will* experience life transformation. This is the incidental transformation discussed in Chapter 5. But, you can intentionally join God in your transforming work by participating in a wide range of spiritual activities:

- Learn to study the Bible for yourself.
- Apply one lesson from each sermon.
- Memorize a Bible verse each week.
- Pray daily. Confess your sin and thank God for His blessings.
- Attend Celebrate Recovery or a similar ministry.
- Start journaling your thoughts about God and life.
- Begin giving to God each week.
- Read excellent Christian books about God or the spiritual life.
- Maintain the Sabbath by practicing true rest.
- Pray for others.
- Attend a special seminar or conference at your church.
- Practice the spiritual discipline of fasting.
- Reconcile conflict with others.
- Teach someone else what you are learning about God.
- Sign up for a weekend retreat.

None of these things are guaranteed to produce spiritual transformation. But, they facilitate the transformation God wants to do in a person's life. When you participate in spiritually enriching activities, you make yourself available for God's greater work.

**From Transformation to Beyond into My Church:** Those who are changed by God are sent by God to change their world. This begins in the church. You are already a member of your church (Belong to Church), but you may not have started serving in your church. Discover your spiritual gift(s) and learn what ministry opportunities are available at your church. Attend whatever training might be necessary for ministry success and begin serving faithfully. Keep your ears open to occasional needs that arise. Help your church succeed in its Gospel mission.

**From Church to Neighborhood:** It's time to venture out into the mission field God has prepared especially *for you*. Meet your neighbors, remember their names and pray for them when you take your evening walk. Ask your coworkers or the cashier you meet at the market how you can pray for them. Keep your ears attuned to needs among people around you—help with moving, meals after surgery, babysitting for an anniversary dinner, lawn care while they're on vacation or an extra hand on a project proposal. Attend wedding, funerals and life events. Look for opportunities to talk about Jesus as the reason for your hope. Remember, the Gospel is demonstration as well as proclamation.

**From Neighborhood to World:** The more sensitive you become to the needs in your neighborhood, the more you will become sensitive to the needs of the world who has never heard about Jesus. Begin supporting a missionary through your church. Invite visiting missionaries to dinner to share their story. Pray for the nations at the evening meal. Attend the Perspectives on the World Christian Movement seminar if it comes to your area. Watch documentaries on remote regions of the world. Befriend international students at your local university. Help a refugee resettle in America. Dare to go on a short-term mission trip overseas.

## Remember Where You're Going

By now, you have taken personal inventory about where you are and have identified practical steps you can take to make spiritual progress along the pathway. However, as you go, you must remember where you are going. The goal of the spiritual pathway isn't religion or church attendance. It isn't even maturity for the sake of maturity. The goal is missional living for the sake of God's glory. We belong to Jesus Christ, biblical community and church in order to be changed by God. We are changed by God to change our church, our neighborhood and our world. Notice that the penultimate goal is our life change to accomplish the greater goal of changing our world. All of this is because we believe God is infinitely worthwhile for others to meet and know. So, the ultimate goal of our spiritual journey is the exaltation of our great God. We must keep this in mind.

## Walking in Circles

So far, we have talked about the spiritual pathway as if it is a linear journey, with a starting step and a final step at the end. But, the normal spiritual life is really an ongoing cycle. In some ways, it's like attending school. When a child finishes third grade, they're not at the end of their educational journey. Rather, they're now qualified to move to a higher level of learning. In the fourth grade, they experience more difficult math, reading and science—the same subjects they studied a year earlier, but now at a different level.

Similarly, the Christian who BELONGS to Christ, community and church and then begins to experience real life transformation (BECOME) doesn't cease to BELONG. In fact, the more life transformation they experience, the more necessary it is for them to connect deeply with Jesus and other believers. In the same way, the further we go on mission (BEYOND), the more life transformation we experience and the more we cling to Jesus and crave Christian fellowship. Our missional journey is never complete until we appear in the presence of the Lord and hear Him say, "Well done, good and faithful servant."

## Mission Possible

As I neared the finish of this book, I received an email from a lady who had been attending our church for some time. It's not uncommon for me to receive a note from someone expressing appreciation for something they have experienced through our ministry. But, this letter was particularly gratifying. As you read it, consider how this family has "walked" the spiritual pathway over a year:

*Dear Pastor David,*

*I wanted to write to you to show my appreciation and how blessed my family is to have found Pantego Bible Church. My husband, Kyle, and I, along with our 2 year-old son, starting attending Pantego Bible Church in February 2015 and could not believe how easy it was to connect in our new church. My husband and I grew up with different church backgrounds: He grew up in a traditional small-town Church of Christ and I grew up in a home where we didn't go to church and only knew about Jesus from sporadically attending church with friends. I didn't think we would find a church that would meet what we were both needed. After visiting several different churches in the area, it only took one visit to know that Pantego Bible Church was perfect for us.*

*We joined a Sunday morning Community Group Bible Study where we were welcomed with open arms to an amazing group of people.*

When we learned about evening Home Groups, we didn't think we would be able to find a group that had the same crazy schedule as we did, was in our region of the city and that could meet on weekends. God answered our prayers with a couple who invited us to their Home Group not far from where we lived that met on Sunday nights.

I joined the "Bible in a Year" Bible Study and, even though I started six months late, I was welcomed like a longtime friend. The women in my group were so open and guided me with my daily reading and helped me understand God's Word. I can now say I have read half of the Bible! Some may not think of it as a great accomplishment, but to me it was something I never imagined I could do. God showed me I had the patience and commitment to read His Word and I have continued reading the "first half" of my Bible and determined to finish the rest. Kyle joined the "A Man and His Design" Bible Study and was so encouraged by the message it brought.

God has blessed us in so many ways since we have joined the church. We have met many amazing people who are now close friends. One of those friends encouraged me to get baptized at the church baptism service in October. This was something I had struggled with for years since becoming a Christian in high school. I frequently felt like I was missing something, but wasn't sure what I should do. The whole month of October, I felt God telling me to do it and I am so glad I listened to Him and to my friend. My relationship with God this year has been the best it's ever been and I hope as my family and I continue to grow our relationship with God, it will be at Pantego Bible Church.

With all of the blessing God has given us this year, we were able to give back more than ever. God gave us the opportunity to bless others by sponsoring a Compassion International child, filling shoeboxes for Samaritan's Purse's Operation Christmas Child and adopting a child from the Angel Tree at Christmas. Last year, we struggled financially and we expected this year would be the same. But at every struggle, God was there. Even last night, my husband said that God truly carried us financially this year.

This year has been one of the greatest years for my family. I thank God every day for guiding us to our church. I thank you and your staff for creating a church environment that spreads God's Word the way He intended and is so giving to communities no matter how far away they *are. I look forward for the year 2016 and what God has in store for both my family and Pantego Bible Church.*

*Blessings,*
*Amanda Bray*

Hopefully, you were able to follow Amanda's journey as she and her family followed the spiritual pathway plotted for her through the ministries of our church. First, she was able to connect with others in meaningful relationships found in our Community Groups and Home Groups (BELONG). They discovered friends which whom they could do life together.

Next, Amanda and Kyle began to enjoy life transformation (BECOME) through Bible studies, among many things. Their hearts and minds and lives were changed as they studied God's Word. As Amanda grew in her personal love for the Lord, she was finally led to be obedient in baptism.

Finally, the Brays learned to go BEYOND. They surrendered their financial offerings to the Lord and got personally involved in sponsoring an impoverished child somewhere in the world and providing Christmas gifts for local children in need. Even better, they are looking for more in the year ahead.

This is just one example of how the spiritual pathway looks in real life. Each person's journey will be as unique as they are. But, each journey will find expressions of connection, transformation and mission.

## Finish the Race

A story of remarkable resolve unfolded in the 1968 Olympics in Mexico City. Tanzanian runner, John Stephen Akhwari, was almost halfway through the marathon race when his body began to cramp up. Pressing on, he jockeyed for course position and was hit, tumbling to the track and dislocating his knee. But the runner wouldn't quit. As the sun set in Mexico and spectators left the stadium, Akhwari crossed the finish line in last place, a full hour behind the Ethiopian winner. As he finished, a cheer rose from the small crowd and television reporters gathered around the African, wondering why he persevered when there was no hope of winning. Akhwari's response was unforgettable: "My country did not send me 5,000 miles to *start* the race; they sent me 5,000 miles to *finish* the race."

As a Christian, my goal is to finish the calling God has on my life. I am inspired by the Apostle Paul who, on his third missionary journey, was in a hurry to reach Jerusalem. He knew that there would be obstacles and distractions that would get in the way of his mission. But, he was undeterred in reaching the goal. He states, *However, I consider my life worth nothing to me, if only I may finish the race and complete the task the Lord Jesus has given me—the task of testifying to the gospel of God's grace.* (Acts 20:24). He knew that God had not sent him to start, but to finish the race.

Paul's "mission statement" in this verse highlights several characteristics of a missional disciple that keep them running the race. First, missional disciples are surrendered to God's purposes. They consider their own life "worth nothing" to themselves. In Philippians 3:7, Paul wrote, *"But, whatever was to my profit I now consider loss for the sake of Christ."* He had surrendered himself fully to Jesus and His plans. A missional disciple is God-centered, not self-centered. They are ever-asking, "What is the Lord's will?" and "Will God be glorified in my decision?" Unlike the leader who is constantly trying to save their life, build their ministry, or magnify their reputation, the missional disciple is most fulfilled in giving their life away. In them, the words of Jesus prove true: *"For whoever wants to save his life will lose it, but whoever loses his life for me will find it"* (Matthew 16:25).

Second, missional disciples are single-minded in God's calling. They are eager to "finish the race and complete the task" they have been given. I ran a half-marathon several years ago through the city streets of Dallas, Texas. Along the race route, I passed coffee shops and water stations, both offering something for my thirst. But, only the water stations set up by the event organizers served the purpose of keeping me running. If I had stopped at a coffee shop, I would have become distracted from finishing the race.

Everything a disciple encounters in life is either moving them further down the track or getting them sidetracked from their goal. This includes the books they read, the way they spend their free time, the relationships they cultivate, the responsibilities they assume and the things they buy. Everything either helps them reach their destination of serving God or becomes a distraction to that end.

Amy Carmichael was a missionary to India for 55 years. Her work among young girls forced into Hindu temple prostitution is immeasurable. When she considered the possibility of retiring, she wrote, "The vows of God are upon me. I may not stay to play with shadows or pluck earthly flowers, till my work I have done and rendered up account." She believed that she should never detour from the race she was running until she crossed the finish line.

Finally, missional disciples are moved by grace. Paul knew firsthand the impact of God's grace upon his life and he wished to share "amazing grace" with others. The ministry leader isn't compelled by duty or personal ambition. Having experienced God's grace personally, they wish for others to encounter the kindness of God which forgives and sets people free.

So, my friends, continue to return to God's overflowing well of grace. Recall who you *were* and who you are, all because of grace. Remember God's calling on your life—not because you were exceptionally qualified, but because our exceptional God uses flawed servants. Rejoice that your significance isn't based on any success you manage in ministry, but based on Jesus' completed work on your behalf. And, reflect on the possibility that the same grace that changed you can change *anyone* else in your world. May grace inspire your heart and motivate you to finish the race God has given to you!

## Our Mission

The mission of Pantego Bible Church is "Making God known by making disciples who are changed by God to change their world." We are a Kingdom-minded church committed to training leaders and laypeople through the generous surrender of all our resources. Your purchase of this book has provided for one or more free copies of this book or the companion volume, *Next Step Church*, to international ministry leaders. If you believe this book would encourage your spiritual walk, but cannot afford it, we will gladly give you one.

To make a contribution to our global leadership training of this 3B Spiritual Pathway, please contact us at 3B@pantego.org. To learn more about our church, please visit us online at pantego.org.

**Pantego Bible Church**
8001 Anderson Boulevard
Fort Worth, Texas 76120
817-274-1315
www.pantego.org

David Daniels has served as Lead Pastor at Pantego Bible Church in Fort Worth, Texas since 2005. Prior to this position, he served at churches in Austin, Texas and Bloomington, Minnesota. David has a Bachelor of Fine Arts from The University of Texas at Austin, a Master of Divinity from Denver Seminary and a Doctor of Ministry from Dallas Theological Seminary.

David is co-founder of Beta Upsilon Chi (Brothers Under Christ), a national Christian fraternity. His commitment to personal discipleship, leadership development and global missions has taken him and his family around the world on short-term trips. David's teaching and training ministry includes the *Perspectives on the World Christian Movement*, Pine Cove Christian Camps, Kanakuk Institute and the Love4Life Marriage Mini-Conference which he co-developed in 2009. He is also an article contributor for the 2011 *Quest Study Bible*.

David's personal mission statement —"Making God famous by making disciples who are changed by God to change their world"—expresses his vision of life transformation that ends in the ultimate goal of God's glory. His life verse is Acts 20:24 —"*However, I consider my life worth nothing to me, if only I may finish the race and complete the task the Lord Jesus has given me—the task of testifying to the gospel of God's grace.*"

David and his wife, Tiffany, live in Arlington, Texas and enjoy life with their children, Grant (and wife, Laine), Pearson and Jenna. You may connect with David on Facebook, Instagram or Twitter (pastor_daniels) or email him directly at ddaniels@pantego.org.

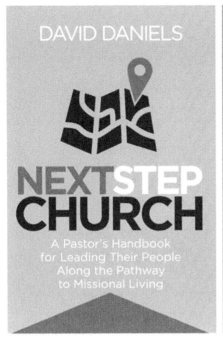
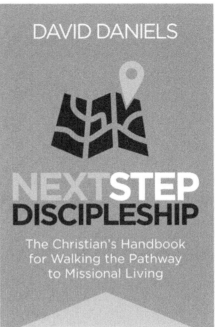

*Next Step Church* is the pastor's handbook to lead people along the pathway to greater missional living. This volume includes chapters to help the pastor discern their calling, give attention to their personal care and understand their ministry commission. It is a valuable resource for new pastors, bi-vocational leaders and pastors around the world who would benefit from foundational ministry training.

*Next Step Discipleship* is the Christian's personal handbook to walk the pathway to greater missional living. It is designed to help the believer discern where they are in their spiritual journey and take next steps to greater ministry effectiveness.

Both resources are available online at amazon.com. Contact Pantego Bible Church for volume discounts at pantego.org or email 3B@pantego.org.

Made in the USA
Monee, IL
31 July 2021